Routledge Questions & Answers

Medical Law
2013–2014

Routledge Q&A series

Each Routledge Q&A contains approximately 50 questions on topics commonly found on exam papers, with comprehensive suggested answers. The titles are written by lecturers who are also examiners, so the student gains an important insight into exactly what examiners are looking for in an answer. This makes them excellent revision and practice guides. With over 500,000 copies of the Routledge Q&As sold to date, accept no other substitute.

New editions publishing in 2013:

Civil Liberties & Human Rights
Company Law
Commercial Law
Constitutional & Administrative Law
Contract Law
Criminal Law
Employment Law
English Legal System
Equity & Trusts
European Union Law

Evidence
Family Law
Jurisprudence
Land Law
Medical Law
Torts

Published in 2012:

Business Law 2012–2013
Intellectual Property Law 2012–2013

For a full listing, visit **http://cw.routledge.com/textbooks/revision**

Routledge Questions & Answers Series

Medical Law

2013–2014

Jonathan Herring

Professor of Law, Exeter College, Oxford and author of numerous books on criminal law, family law and medical law and ethics

Routledge
Taylor & Francis Group

LONDON AND NEW YORK

Second edition published 2013
by Routledge
2 Park Square, Milton Park, Abingdon, Oxon OX14 4RN

Simultaneously published in the USA and Canada
by Routledge
711 Third Avenue, New York, NY 10017

Routledge is an imprint of the Taylor & Francis Group, an informa business

First edition published by Routledge 2011

British Library Cataloguing-in-Publication Data
A catalogue record for this book is available from the British Library

Library of Congress Cataloging-in-Publication Data
Herring, Jonathan.
    Medical law / Jonathan Herring. — 2nd ed.
        p. cm.—(Q&A, Routledge questions & answers series)
    ISBN 978–0–415–69974–7 (pbk)—ISBN 978–0–203–08379–6 (ebk)
    1. Medical laws and legislation—England—Examinations, questions, etc.   I. Title.
    KD3395.H473 2013
    344.4204′1076—dc23

                                                                                2012018943

ISBN: 978–0–415–69974–7 (pbk)
ISBN: 978–0–203–08379–6 (ebk)

Typeset in TheSans
by RefineCatch Limited, Bungay, Suffolk

Printed and bound in Great Britain by the MPG Books Group

Contents

Table of Cases

Table of Legislation

STATUTES

STATUTORY INSTRUMENTS

EUROPEAN AND INTERNATIONAL LEGISLATION

Guide to the Companion Website

http://cw.routledge.com/textbooks/revision

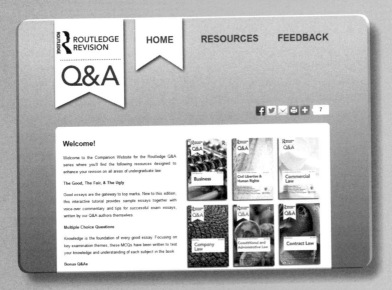

Visit the Routledge Q&A website to discover even more study tips and advice on getting those top marks.

On the Routledge revision website you will find the following resources designed to enhance your revision on all areas of undergraduate law.

The Good, The Fair, & The Ugly

Good essays are the gateway to top marks. This interactive tutorial provides sample essays together with voice-over commentary and tips for successful exam essays, written by our Q&A authors themselves.

Multiple Choice Questions

Knowledge is the foundation of every good essay. Focusing on key examination themes, these MCQs have been written to test your knowledge and understanding of each subject in the book.

Bonus Q&As

Having studied our exam advice, put your revision into practice and test your essay writing skills with our additional online questions and answers.

Don't forget to check out even more revision guides and exam tools from Routledge!

Lawcards

Lawcards are your complete, pocket-sized guides to key examinable areas of the undergraduate law.

Routledge Student Statutes

Comprehensive selections; clear, easy-to-use layout; alphabetical, chronological, and thematic indexes; and a competitive price make *Routledge Student Statutes* the statute book of choice for the serious law student.

Introduction

Exams in medical law usually involve two kinds of questions: essay questions and problem questions. There are normally more essay questions than problem ones, and that is reflected in this book.

To do really well in a medical law exam you need to show a good understanding of the law (of course!) but also a good knowledge of the ethical principles. This can worry students: should I be spending more time writing about ethics or more time writing about law? Your lecturer may have given you specific guidance on this. For most courses it is important to make sure you include both. An essay which is full of cases but fails to mention a single ethical argument is unlikely to do well. But neither would an essay which cited many great ethicists, but neglected to refer to a single case.

Your examiner is likely to give you some leeway: so as long as there is a reasonable mixture of law and ethics she or he will not mind if you have slightly more ethics or slightly more law. The best answers will integrate both law and ethics, showing how the legal principles reflect (or do not reflect) ethical principles, or discuss how a particular case reveals a clash between different ethical approaches.

When discussing ethical issues, try where possible to refer to particular commentators. So saying 'John Harris argues . . .' is preferable to 'It might be argued . . .'. It is not always possible to cite an author for a particular view, but where you can, do so. This will show the examiner that you have read the material set and you are aware of the academic debates.

One final point. Medical law is great fun and part of the reason for that is that it raises controversial issues. Understandably students get worked up over some issues and have strong views. So they should. But do not let this affect your exam performance. First, make sure that you keep your discussion located in the legal and ethical writings. Do not go off on a rant of your own! Second, refer to the arguments on both sides of the debate. A good argument will always explain not only the reasons in favour of its view, but also why the arguments against it are bad. But always be respectful. Don't dismiss particular views in contemptuous terms. After all, you don't know what the examiner's views are. Anyway, rudeness and lack of respect are inappropriate for a lawyer. So treat others' views in a serious and polite way. That said, don't be afraid of stating your convictions. A wishy-washy essay which expresses no opinion is not going to excite the examiner!

Common Pitfalls

The most common mistake made when using Questions & Answers books for revision is to memorise the model answers provided and try to reproduce them in exams. This approach is a sure-fire pitfall, likely to result in a poor overall mark because your answer will not be specific enough to the particular question on your exam paper, and there is also a danger that reproducing an answer in this way would be treated as plagiarism. You must instead be sure to read the question carefully, to identify the issues and problems it is asking you to address and to answer it directly in your exam. If you take our examiners' advice and use your Q&A to focus on your question-answering skills and understanding of the law applied, you will be ready for whatever your exam paper has to offer!

Medical Negligence

QUESTION 1

Assess the *Bolam* test.

COMMENTARY

The examiner has gone for a short and to the point question here. Remember to look carefully at the wording of the question. Notice that we are asked to assess the test. So it is not just a question of defining it – candidates are required to discuss and analyse it. Notice too that we are asked to assess the *Bolam* test and not the whole of the law of medical negligence. So keep focused on the question asked.

The structure of the essay will be straightforward. The *Bolam* test will be defined. This could take up the whole essay, and given that you are primarily asked to assess the test it is better to keep this discussion brief. Then we will look at some of the criticisms of the test, before looking at some of the alleged advantages. It will then be necessary to consider whether any of the alternatives are preferable. Finally a conclusion will be drawn.

One general point in essays of this kind is that it is easy to lambast a particular legal rule and point out all its flaws; however, unless you can find a better alternative the objections to it will be weaker. Remember, often in difficult legal issues there are competing principles which need to be balanced. Any legal rule will therefore have its drawbacks and benefits. To make a case that the law needs to be reformed you need to show that the proposal has greater benefits and/or fewer drawbacks to the current law.

How to Answer this Question

- ❖ Define the *Bolam* test
- ❖ Set out the advantages
- ❖ Set out the problems with it
- ❖ What alternatives are there?
- ❖ Conclusion.

Answer Structure

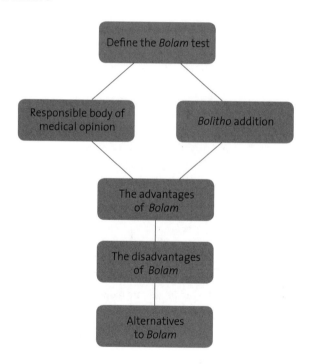

SUGGESTED ANSWER

In order to prove that there has been a case of medical negligence the claimant must show that the medical professional breached the duty of care. Normally in the law of tort that involves asking the simple question: did the defendant behave in a reasonable way? However, the law developed slightly differently in the cases of clinical negligence in which the *Bolam* test is used. In this essay we will set out what the test is and consider the arguments for and against its use.[1]

The *Bolam* test was first set out in *Bolam v Friern HMC* (1957). There it was held:

> A doctor is not guilty of negligence if he has acted in accordance with a practice accepted as proper by a responsible body of medical men skilled in that particular art.

That test has been applied to all medical professionals and is not restricted to doctors. Although *Bolam* was a first instance decision it has been approved on several occasions by the House of Lords, most recently in *Bolitho v City and Hackney HA* (1997).

The significance of the *Bolam* test is that it provides a defence for a doctor to show that there was a responsible body of medical opinion which supported his or her conduct. That body of opinion need not be a majority one. So even if most doctors would describe the conduct of the defendant as negligent, if there is a responsible body which would not, then he or she has a defence. This makes it very difficult for the claimant to show there has been negligence because even though they may find experts who state that the conduct is negligent, unless every responsible expert agrees they are unlikely to succeed. In *Bolitho v City and Hackney HA* the House of Lords emphasised that the body of opinion has to be a responsible one. Therefore finding a rogue doctor who would support the defendant will not provide a defence. Lord Brown-Wilkinson went further by saying that to be responsible the body of opinion must have a logical basis. These *dicta* show that the judges will not necessarily simply accept that because an expert says that the defendant's behaviour was acceptable it cannot be negligent – they will require convincing that such a view is responsible and logical. However, it would be very rare for a judge to declare an expert medical witness either illogical or irresponsible.

Turning now to the objections to the *Bolam* test, first it is claimed that the test means it is the members of the medical profession, rather than the courts, that decide what is reasonable practice. The point is that the *Bolam* test means that the standards of negligence for doctors are very different from those in other walks of life. In a driving case, for example, the court will assess whether a driver lived up to the standards of the reasonable driver and it is no defence for the driver to show that many drivers would have driven in the way he or she did. Opponents claim that what the *Bolam* test ignores is that a responsible body of medical opinion may be misguided or old-fashioned and should then be seen as negligent.

A second objection is that the *Bolam* test makes it very difficult for a claimant to assess their chances of success. They may instruct experts who give strong evidence that the

---

1   This paragraph sets out well the structure of the essay.

conduct is negligent, but they will lose if a single convincing witness is found on the other side. A claimant can only be confident of success if she makes sure she knows about every possible opinion on the behaviour of the defendant. That makes clinical negligence litigation unpredictable. A cynic might even suggest that the law is designed to discourage people from bringing claims.

A third objection is that it is becoming difficult for claimants to find expert medical witnesses who would testify against their colleagues. It is one thing to be asked in court to testify that the way a colleague behaved was sub-standard and that they were not behaving as a reasonable doctor. It is another matter to say the way they behaved was below the standard of how any reasonable doctor would have behaved.

These objections will be responded to by supporters of the *Bolam* test, who tend to make the following points. First, judges are simply not in a position to resolve a dispute between two groups of expert doctors over the best way to treat a particular condition. The judge will know less about medicine than either group of experts. So saying, as the *Bolam* test does, that there is no negligence if a responsible body of opinion supports the defendant, the law acknowledges this. The law in effect is saying, 'Well, there are two groups of medical experts who disagree on this and we cannot choose who is right.' While a judge is normally in a position to readily determine whether or not a driver was acting reasonably, he or she is a pure amateur in relation to medical issues. The strength of this response is weakened by the fact that judges do regularly choose between expert opinions in relation to other areas of life, from computer programming to sheep breeding, even though they are amateurs in such matters. Judges regularly choose which expert on computer programming or farming they agree with.[2]

This leads to a second and more convincing argument in favour of *Bolam*. That is that the *Bolam* test acknowledges and encourages innovative and exciting medical practice. It is commendable that doctors are trying out new treatments (as long as they are carried out under the appropriate guidelines). Consider, for example, the work of Wendy Savage, who did much to promote a woman-centred approach to gynaecology. At the time her practices were seen as unorthodox, but now they would be standard. If the *Bolam* test were different she would have been open to being sued early in her career, and the advances she promoted might not have been made. This argument might explain why medical treatment is different from other situations. We don't want drivers trying out unorthodox methods of driving cars; nor bricklayers departing from standard bricklaying practice; but we do want doctors to try out new treatments, as long as they follow the regulations governing medical research.

---

2   The examiners like it if you can show an awareness not just of medical law, but other subjects you have studied.

A third point that supporters might make is that *Bolam* does discourage litigation but that is preferable because the NHS is already under significant financial strain, without facing the extra costs of litigation.[3] Without the *Bolam* test litigation would get out of control, threatening the existence of the NHS itself. Of course, that does not necessarily follow. Maybe without the *Bolam* test doctors would be more careful.

Overall, the arguments seem well balanced. The test certainly makes it difficult to sue. However, it means that patients might receive no compensation for injuries caused by unorthodox medicine because the defendant is able to find a small group of doctors who would support what he or she did. It certainly makes it harder for a claimant to establish a case of negligence. On the other hand, the test provides protection for a doctor who is seeking to depart from the standard approach to a medical problem and trying an innovative technique. It may be that the approach heralded by *Bolitho* is the way forward, namely to stick with the *Bolam* test but encourage the courts to be more sceptical about claims that there is a responsible body of medical opinion supporting an approach which clearly appears inappropriate.

So what could replace the *Bolam* test?[4] We could use the straightforward test for negligence: did the doctor act in a reasonable way? That will make it difficult for the judge to resolve a case where there are two medical experts who disagree on the correct approach to a particular condition. It is understandable in such a case that the judge may feel that he or she lacks the expertise to make the assessment. However, that is a common aspect of the judicial role. More concerning is that such a test may work against an innovative doctor who is attempting a pioneering approach to medical treatment.

Another alternative would be to move to a no-fault system of clinical negligence. We do not have the space to discuss that in detail. It should be noted, however, that the Government recently decided that moving to such a scheme would simply be too expensive. In the current economic climate it is hard to imagine a government wanting to adopt such an approach.

To conclude, in this essay we have set out the definition of the *Bolam* test. We have described some of the objections to it, and some of the arguments in its support. Overall, despite its many flaws the *Bolam* test seems the best available, as long as the courts take a robust approach in determining whether or not the defendant's actions really were supported by a responsible body of opinion and by ensuring that the test is not used as a way of hiding inadequate work.[5]

....

3 Here you can show you are thinking about the practical issues, as well as the legal ones, which will please the examiner.
4 Remember it is no good just criticising a law. A good essay will then consider what alternatives would be preferable.
5 There is a good summary of the main points made in the essay, bringing the essay to a satisfying conclusion.

QUESTION 2

Alex comes to the accident and emergency room complaining of a very bad headache. He is seen by Doctor Sue. The accident and emergency room is very busy that night and Sue only has time for a quick check-up of Alex. She gives him a few painkillers and sends him home. She has failed to notice that Alex has a serious brain injury and he dies from it a few days later. Expert evidence shows that had Sue correctly diagnosed the problem an effective treatment would have been available.

Bertha is also at the accident and emergency room, with a rash. Doctor Sue asks Nurse Tom to see Bertha as she is so busy. Tom fails to spot that Bertha is suffering from meningitis and sends her home with some cream. She later dies from the meningitis. Tom has only recently started work as a nurse. The evidence suggests that had Tom spotted the condition there was a 45 per cent chance that treatment would have been effective to treat the meningitis. However, had Bertha been seen soon after her arrival in the accident and emergency room there would have been a 55 per cent chance of effective treatment.

❱ Assess whether Sue or Tom are liable for negligence.

COMMENTARY

This is a problem question concerning two professionals: Sue and Tom. Remember to always look carefully at what you are being asked to discuss in a problem question. Sometimes you are invited to discuss the general legal issues that arise, but in this case you are asked specifically to address whether they will be liable for negligence. Notice that this excludes a number of issues you might be tempted to discuss: any liability under criminal law; the level of damages awarded; or breach of professional guidelines.

Looking first of all at Alex's case, the key issue will be the application of the *Bolam* test. You will need to correctly state the *Bolam* test, but also show the examiner you are aware of the recent developments in the *Bolam* test. In the suggested answer an attempt is made to show how there are tensions in some of the more recent cases on *Bolam*. Notice too that the *Bolam* test operates in the circumstances the person was in and so the hurried nature of the situation needs to be considered.

Moving on to Bertha's case we need to consider Tom's liability. Remember that the *Bolam* test applies to all medical professionals. Even if he was liable, notice that there was only a

45 per cent chance that a treatment would be available. This will require you to consider the 'loss of chance' cases (e.g. *Gregg v Scott* (2005)). Another issue to consider here, and one which a lot of candidates will overlook, is that Sue may be liable for the harm to Bertha. Was it negligent of her not to see Bertha herself?

How to Answer this Question

- ❖ Alex: was Sue negligent? Apply the *Bolam* test. Consider the recent case law developments on negligence.
- ❖ Bertha: was Tom negligent? How will the *Bolam* test apply in his case? Is it relevant that he has just started his job?
- ❖ Bertha: was Sue negligent? Was she negligent in delegating the case to Tom?
- ❖ Bertha: discuss the loss of chance issues.

Applying the Law

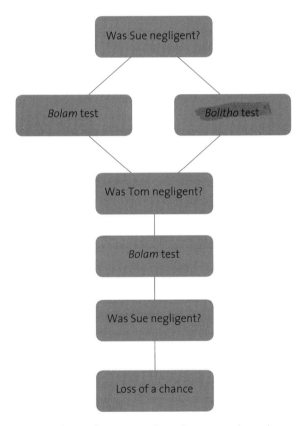

The main factors to consider in relation to Sue's negligence are shown here.

SUGGESTED ANSWER   --------------------------------

We will first consider the case of Alex.[6] If his estate wishes to sue for negligence, they will need to establish that Sue owed Alex a duty of care; that she breached the duty of care; and that the breach of the duty caused the loss. There can be no doubt that Sue owed Alex a duty of care. The primary question is whether there was a breach of the duty.

The court would apply the *Bolam* test. In *Bolam v Friern HMC* (1957) it was held:

> A doctor is not guilty of negligence if he has acted in accordance with a practice accepted as proper by a responsible body of medical men skilled in that particular art.

This means that to find Sue negligent the court would need to be persuaded that there was no responsible body of medical opinion which would see her failure to diagnose as inadequate practice. The *Bolam* test was approved by the House of Lords in *Bolitho v City and Hackney HA* (1997). There are a number of more detailed points appropriate in its application to Sue's case.

First, the *Bolam* test appears to suggest that Sue will have a defence if she can refer to a respectable body of opinion which would say her failure to diagnose the brain injury was acceptable. This need not be a majority opinion or even a large one. In *Defreitas v O'Brien* (1996) it appeared there were only four or five experts in the country who agreed with the way the defendant handled the case.[7] As that was sufficient to amount to a responsible body of opinion the negligence claim failed. However, the issue must now be considered in the light of *Bolitho v City and Hackney HA* (1997). In that case Lord Browne-Wilkinson emphasised that just because there is an expert in the court saying that the defendant was not negligent it does not mean that the judge must accept that view. The judge needs to be persuaded that the body of opinion which held that view was responsible and had a logical basis. So even if Sue finds an expert who will give evidence that her failure was not negligent, it is still open to a judge to find that the evidence does not reflect a responsible body of medical opinion. There is some debate over how open judges will be to making such a finding following *Bolitho*. In *Marriott v West Midlands HA* (1998) a GP prescribed painkillers, rather than ordering tests to see if a patient had a blood clot. Although most GPs would have ordered tests there was evidence in the court that some would not have, as clots are rare. This was rejected by the trial judge and Court of Appeal on the basis that, although clots were rare, if they were found, death or other serious consequences could follow. It would not be responsible not to carry out the tests. This suggests a fairly robust approach to claims about what responsible doctors would do.

....

6   In a problem question it is crucial to have a clear structure and that you make it clear whose claim against whom you are discussing.

7   Here you can show a good knowledge of the case law, but giving an example of a case which applied the *Bolam* test.

However, in other cases a less interventionist approach appears. In *Wisniewski v Central Manchester Health Authority* (1998) the Court of Appeal refused an appeal against a dismissal of negligence claim. The judge had heard an eminent expert give evidence that there was a responsible body of opinion supporting the doctor. Brooke LJ suggested it would be 'quite impossible' to argue that an eminent doctor was not logical. In *Birch v University College London Hospital* (2008) it was held to be rare for a judge to find the views of a medical expert not responsible or illogical. So if Sue is able to find an eminent doctor who confirms that the failure to make the diagnosis was acceptable then she is likely to win the case.[8]

Another issue which will be relevant in this case is that the standard expected will take into account the situation the professional found themselves in. In this case the question will be what standard was acceptable for a doctor in a busy accident and emergency ward with many patients to deal with. There may be a claim against the NHS Trust for failing to ensure adequate staffing at the ward, but that would be a difficult claim to make (see *Garcia v St Mary's NHS Trust* (2006)). However, Sue may well in this case succeed in arguing that, although given plenty of time, she should have discovered the brain injury, given the many patients who were needing her care she acted reasonably.

If it is concluded that Sue was negligent then in this case it seems clear that the negligence caused the death.[9] But for the negligence it is likely that treatment would have been provided and that Alex would have lived.

Turning now to Bertha's case. First, Tom's liability will be discussed. There is little doubt that he owes Bertha a duty of care. Whether there is a breach of duty is less clear. The *Bolam* test will apply; that has already been discussed. But there are two points to emphasise. The first is that Tom will be judged by the standards expected of a nurse, not a consultant (*Stockdale v Nicholls* (1993)). So the issue will be whether there is a responsible body of opinion among the nursing profession that it would be expected of him to spot this diagnosis. However, the fact that he is inexperienced will not be taken into account. He or she will be held to act in the capacity in which he or she is acting. So, in this case Tom will be judged by the reasonable nurse, not the reasonable inexperienced nurse (*Judge v Huntingdon HA* (1995)). In assessing this, one issue the court considers is whether he ought to have checked what he had done with a more senior member of staff (*Horton v Evans* (2006)). The court in considering these questions will take into account professional guidance or the guidance the hospital has issued (*Barnet v Chelsea and*

---

8   After quite a lengthy discussion it is helpful to come to a concise summary of the legal position. Don't worry that you cannot say for sure Sue will win or not. The examiner realises that you often need more information before giving a definitive view.

9   Here it is right to proceed with the discussion on the basis that Sue is negligent. Although it may well be found she is not, the examiner will want you to explain the legal consequences if she is.

Kensington HMC (1968)). If that has not been followed a medical professional is likely to be found to be negligent.[10]

Assuming Tom's liability is established, the next issue is whether a loss is caused by the breach. In this case had Tom made the correct diagnosis there was only a 45 per cent chance of a successful treatment. This is a loss of a chance case. The House of Lords considered this issue in *Gregg v Scott* (2005), where it was held that unless there was a greater than 50 per cent chance of a successful treatment following a misdiagnosis a claim would not lie. This is because it has not been shown that the negligence caused the loss. Even had the correct diagnosis been made it seems most likely that death would still have resulted.

We also need to consider a claim that Sue was negligent in asking Tom to deal with the case. There would be no difficulty in establishing a duty of care. However, the question of breach is tricky. Again the *Bolam* test would apply. If it could be shown that in the case of serious headaches there is no responsible body of medical opinion that would leave diagnosis to a nurse then Sue might be liable. Much would then turn on the timing. If the reasonable doctor would have seen Tom and have done so in time to be able to provide him with treatment with a greater than 50 per cent chance of success then a claim of liability would lie against Sue.

> **Common Pitfalls**
>
> Don't make the assumption that, under the *Bolam* test, if a single doctor can be found to support the defendant she is not negligent. The courts insist that there must be a responsible body of opinion.

QUESTION 3

Consider the issues raised by *Chester v Afshar*.

COMMENTARY

It is not common for an exam question to focus on a single case. However, an examiner might ask you to look at one case where it is a leading decision. If you face a question like this, you will need to put the case in context. Don't think that just because an examiner has only mentioned one case, you don't need to mention any other. You will want to mention the cases that were decided before this case and, where appropriate, cases decided after this case.

There were two key issues addressed in *Chester*. The first is what kind of risks must be disclosed to a patient. You will want to be clear about the issue that is being addressed

---

10   This paragraph is bringing in lots of cases, which will impress the examiner.

here. Remember that in some cases the failure to inform the patient of a risk will mean that the patient is not able to give consent. In that case a battery is committed. In *Chester* we are dealing with cases where some information is provided, enough for there to be consent, but still below the standard expected of the reasonable doctor. So make sure you focus correctly on the issue to address.

The second question in the case was one of causation: did the failure to warn of the risks cause the loss. This has proved a controversial issue and you will need to explain carefully what was decided. Notice that the examiner has asked you to consider the issues raised by the case. So, you will be expected to express a view on whether the court reached the correct conclusion.

How to Answer this Question
❖   Set out the facts of the decision.
❖   Explain the context of the decision and the key questions to be considered.
❖   What information did the House of Lords say needed to be disclosed?
❖   Consider the causation issue raised in *Chester*.
❖   What issues does the case raise which will need to be discussed in the future?

Answer Structure

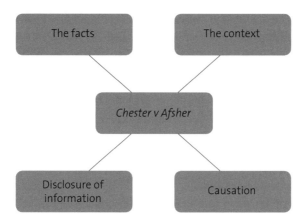

This mind map on Chester v Afshar *illustrates the key points to consider in your answer.*

SUGGESTED ANSWER
The central facts in the decision of *Chester v Afshar* were these. Ms Chester suffered back pain. Mr Afshar, her surgeon, proposed surgery. He failed, however, to disclose that there was a 1–2 per cent risk of significant nerve damage which was an inevitable risk of the surgery. Ms Chester agreed to the operation and although it was performed perfectly properly the risk of nerve damage materialised and she was left partially paralysed. The

trial judge found that had Mr Afshar informed Ms Chester of the risk she would not have consented to the operation at that time, but would have sought a further opinion. However, on receiving the further opinion she would have consented to the treatment probably with Mr Afshar at a later date. The trial judge held that it had therefore been shown there was a causal link between the surgeon's advice and the loss to the patient. The case went up to the House of Lords.[11]

There were two main issues the case raises. The first was whether there was a duty to disclose the risk. It is important to be clear what the question was.

There are two legal issues which can arise in a case where a medical professional has failed to provide information to a patient before treatment. The first is a potential claim of battery. If the patient does not understand the nature of the treatment in general terms then there is no effective consent and the tort of battery may be committed (*Chatterton v Gerson* (1981)). The second is a claim of negligence. This will involve accepting that the patient had enough information to be able to consent, but argue that the medical professional was negligent in failing to act as a reasonable professional would in supplying the correct information to the patient. It was the second of these questions which their lordships had to address.[12]

Before*Chester* the leading case had been*Sidaway v Bethlem RHG* (1985) . The House of Lords unfortunately did not speak clearly with one voice. It seems the majority (Lords Diplock, Bridge and Keith) held that the*Bolam* test dealt with the issue. So the question is simply whether there was a responsible body of opinion which would have thought the amount of information provided was sufficient. Lord Woolf, in the subsequent Court of Appeal decision of*Pearce v United Bristol Healthcare NHS Trust* (1998) , took the view that, although the basic *Bolam* test applied where a party sought to argue that it was not negligent to disclose a serious risk, that view may be found not to be reasonable or responsible. Indeed, as a general principle he suggested that if there were a significant risk that would affect the judgment of the reasonable patient then normally that would need to be disclosed.

Perhaps surprisingly, their lordships dicussion of the issue in*Chester v Afshar* (2004) was brief. Lord Steyn held that the failure to warn of the risk was negligent. He did not use the terminology of the*Bolam* test. Instead, he talked about the duty to warn the patient of serious possible risks. Indeed, he argued that a patient had a right to be informed of small risks of serious injury. This suggests that the courts are moving away from*Bolam* towards an approach that focuses on whether the significant risks are disclosed.

---

11 You would not normally want to set out the facts of a case in so much detail, but because this is the case at the heart of the essay, that is appropriate.

12 Students often overlook this important distinction and it is essential to understanding the case. It is good to reassure the examiner you understand this key distinction.

The second issue was whether the failure to inform Ms Chester of the risk had caused her to suffer the injury. By a majority of three to two their Lordships decided it had. It was held that where a patient had not been warned about a risk of injury and as a result of that failure underwent the operation which she would not have undertaken *at that time* if she had been properly informed, a patient was entitled to compensation. It was not necessary for Ms Chester to show that she would never have consented to the kind of operation at any time in the future, only that she would not have consented to the operation that took place.[13]

This reasoning has been criticised. As the minority pointed out, if Mr Afshar had told Ms Chester of the risk she would have agreed to the operation, although at a later date. She would therefore have been undertaking an operation with exactly the same chance of causing her an injury as the operation she undertook. Lord Steyn, for the majority, emphasised that, even if the risk of the injury occurring was the same whenever she undertook the operation, she would not have suffered exactly the same injury at the same time that she did if the proper information had been given. However, we do not know that. The truth is that at the time of the defendant's negligence the claimant was, as a result of the non-disclosure, facing exactly the same risk she would have faced had the risk been disclosed.

Interestingly, Lord Steyn accpted that Ms Chester's case was weak under the normal rules of causation. He believed that justice required a modification of the normal approach to causation. The duty on doctors to warn patients of risks was important because it protected the rights of patients to make informed choices about whether, and when and by whom, to be operated upon. To leave the patient uninformed about the risk when they would not have immediately consented to the operation if they had been informed of the risk, would render the duty meaningless. Critics might argue that manipulating the normal rules of causation to achieve what is regarded as justice is inappropriate.[14]

Several issues are left unanswered following this case, which have been addressed by later cases. The first is whether the duty is simply on a doctor to state the risks, or must she ensure they are understood? In *Al Hamwi v Johnston* (2005) it was explained that telling a patient of risks at great speed will not necessarily satisfy the legal obligation. The second is that the obligation to disclose covers not only an obligation to disclose the risks attached to the treatment, but also the possibilities of other treatments (*Birch v University College Hospital* (2008). The third is the question of precisely which risks need not be disclosed. In *Rimmer v General Dental Council* (2011) it was held, applying *Chester,* dental practitioners did not need to disclose risks that were non-existent or not serious, or were not risks (however small) of serious harm.[15]

....

13   This is a tricky issue and so it is worth taking time to explain it clearly.

14   The examiner will be pleased that you are able to present both sides of the argument.

15   Here you are showing the examiner that you are familiar with the most recent case law.

QUESTION 4

Should we have a no-fault system for dealing with medical mishaps?

COMMENTARY

This is a popular issue for an essay question. It is helpful to start by explaining why it is that no-fault is even considered as an option for medical negligence cases. This requires you to summarise the main problems with the current law. Then you can consider the arguments on either side of the debate on no-fault.

It is advantageous to have some material up your sleeve which other students will not have (not literally though!). Notice in the suggested answer that there is a brief discussion of how the no-fault system has fared in New Zealand. That is something many students will not include. Remember too to discuss the Chief Medical Officer's report, which brings us down to earth with a bump. Whatever the benefits of a no-fault system, that report concluded it was simply too expensive.

How to Answer this Question

- ❖ Why no-fault is being considered
- ❖ Arguments in favour of no-fault
- ❖ Arguments against no-fault
- ❖ Lessons from New Zealand
- ❖ Conclusions.

Answer Structure

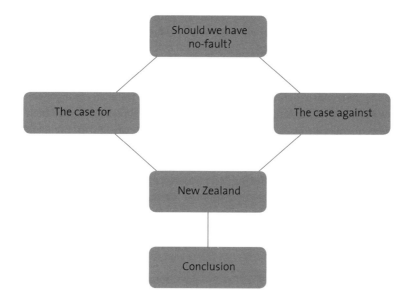

SUGGESTED ANSWER -

There is considerable unease with the current law on medical mishaps. It seems to satisfy no one. The complaints are well documented: the process is slow; it generates enormous legal costs; it creates considerable stress all round; it encourages secrecy rather than openness; it does not encourage learning lessons from mistakes; too many people do not receive compensation when they desperately need it; some people receive more compensation than they need ... And so we could go on. Interestingly, in one survey 70 per cent of claimants reported being totally or very dissatisfied with the system. In fact, the only people who seem rather silent in their opposition are lawyers who work on medical negligence cases!

There have been a number of proposals for reform, including the NHS Redress Act 2006. But in this essay the focus will be on the most radical solution: a no-fault scheme. A patient injured as a result of a medical mishap will receive compensation, whether or not there was negligence. First, the benefits of such a scheme will be considered, before some of the objections to it are examined.[16]

The first benefit is a call to justice. Imagine two patients who are left paralysed after an operation. Under the current system it is quite possible that one will be able to prove negligence and receive substantial compensation to assist in providing care for them, while the other will be left with nothing. There may be no real difference in the condition they suffer from, or their needs, but what might be a matter of luck in finding evidence of

- -

16 It is a good idea to explain to the examiner how you intend to tackle the question.

negligence or causation can have huge ramifications. Or, more cynically, the outcome might depend on how honest the doctor is with the patient about what happened. Such arbitrariness in outcome would be avoided under a no-fault system, where both patients would automatically recover the same award.

The second benefit is that the no-fault process would reduce animosity. Gone would be the stress to the doctor of a claim that he or she had behaved improperly; and gone would be the worry for the patient about whether their claim would succeed.[17] Both the doctor and patient could focus on the future and getting the patient better, without creating an adversarial relationship of the kind that negligence claims generate. There is a linked benefit too. The tortuous approach encourages secrecy. Doctors are reluctant to be open about what went wrong for fear that this will be used as evidence that they are negligent. With the no-fault scheme this fear is removed and doctors can be open about what happened, and this can help the NHS learn from its past mistakes. Indeed, the Chief Medical Officer in his report thought this was one of the main defects of the current approach – that it did not encourage the NHS to learn from what went wrong in the past.

A third benefit of the no-fault based system is that we move away from blaming a particular doctor. Under the current system there is much focus on whether a particular professional can be found negligent in the *Bolam* sense. Sometimes the negligence in fact lies in the overall system rather than with the actions of an individual. This can, as already mentioned, mean that lessons are not learned for the future. If the system is at fault, blaming one person and replacing her will not do anyone any good (Merry and McCall Smith[18]).

Finally, the current system is extremely expensive. There are the costs of litigation for individuals and the NHS, which are considerable, and there are the emotional costs too. Doctors who are being sued report high levels of stress and anxiety, as do patients.

We turn now to some of the arguments against a no-fault system. These include the following. First, assuming the scheme is not seeking to compensate everyone who falls ill, we need to find a way of distinguishing medical mishaps and those people who are just ill or suffering the normal side effects of treatment. This will generate considerable complexity. Whether a particular consequence is a risk which is inherent to an operation or is the result of a medical mishap may be very difficult to tell. It might introduce just as much complexity as the current system. Indeed the distinction might, in effect, re-introduce the fault issue into the picture.

Second, a no-fault scheme would lack accountability. One of the aims of tort law is to identify wrongdoers and publicly declare their negligence and require the payment of compensation. Under a no-fault system there would be no recognition that a patient had

---

17   Here you can show the examiner you are aware of the emotional, as well as legal issues involved.
18   A. Merry and A. McCall Smith, *Errors, Medicine and the Law*, Cambridge: Cambridge University Press, 2001.

been wronged, only that they had suffered a loss. It might be argued that the law would thereby lose its moral role. Doctors would no longer be held to account for their wrongdoing. It might even be said to be losing its deterrent effect. This is true and a no-fault system would need to be supported by a system of professional regulation, which if necessary would involve disciplining doctors who behaved wrongly.

Third, and perhaps most significantly, a no-fault system would place a huge financial burden on the Government. The Chief Medical Officer, in his 2003 report, *Making Amends*, estimated that introducing a no-fault scheme would cost at a minimum £1.6 billion a year and could cost up to £28 billion, depending on its exact nature.[19] Especially in the current economic climate, it is very unlikely that such a vast increase in public expenditure could be seen as justified. However, this point should be treated with care. It should be recalled that we are discussing the costs of providing care for individuals. If compensation is not provided it is not as if there is no cost; it is that the cost is borne by the patient and, in particular, those who care for him or her. So the question should not be about 'increased cost' but rather a debate about who should bear that cost.

In the debate on no-fault systems for clinical mishaps, it is helpful to refer to the no-fault system in New Zealand, administered by the Accident Compensation Corporation under the **Injury Prevention, Rehabilitation and Compensation Amendment Act (No. 2) 2005** As its name suggests, the Act is designed not only to provide compensation but also to prevent injuries generally and to encourage rehabilitation. It compensates injuries which are not a necessary part of or an ordinary consequence of medical treatment. So a scar or well-known side effect would not be included. Ken Oliphant in his discussion of the Act notes that the scheme has not encountered huge difficulties in interpretation and that claims are dealt with speedily. He notes that the criticism is made that professionals are not held adequately to account under the scheme. A professional who behaved inappropriately and a professional who just had a misfortune are dealt with in the same way. It is, however, notable that only 3 per cent of those who can claim do so. It may be that the scheme is only affordable because so few people take up the claim. Significantly, of those who do claim 84 per cent are satisfied.[20]

To conclude, the current system has many faults. The main argument against no-fault lies in the expense that falls on the State. But, as argued above, that is an expense that otherwise falls on those disabled by the medical mishaps or on their carers. A fairer distribution of the burdens of medical mishaps could be provided by a no-fault scheme. However, that would

---

19 Where possible, as here, use some precise data to back up your arguments.
20 The examiner will be very impressed if you can draw on international comparisons to make your point, as made here.

need to be supported by an effective system of professional regulation which ensures that incompetent medical professionals are identified and dealt with appropriately.[21]

Aim Higher ★

No-fault systems are often rejected because they cost too much. However, the cost of caring for a seriously ill patient must be carried by someone. If not the State, it will be the individual affected.

---

21 Don't worry if you feel you cannot take a strong view one way or the other. You get no marks for being extreme. This conclusion shows the writer is aware of the complex issues raised.

Rationing

Checklist ✔

You need to be aware of

- The definition of rationing of health care
- The role of the National Institute for Clinical Excellence
- The approach taken by the courts when rationing health care
- The ethical issues raised by health care rationing

QUESTION 5

Assess the role of the courts in considering challenges to decisions about the rationing of medical resources.

COMMENTARY

This is a common approach for an exam question on this topic. What the question is getting at is whether the courts are willing to look at the substance of a rationing decision or whether they only focus on the procedure. There is a major political issue: is it for the courts or the public authorities to determine how rationing decisions are made?

You will need to set out the case law. There is not a huge amount and so that makes it an easy question to revise for. You will also want to show the examiner you are aware of some of the theoretical debates about the roles of the court in this area.

How to Answer this Question

- ❖ Setting the context for rationing decision
- ❖ Statutory obligations
- ❖ Judicial Review claims
- ❖ Human Rights arguments.

Answer Structure

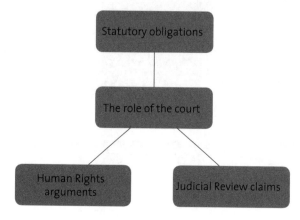

This mind map on the role of the court illustrates the key points to consider in your answer.

SUGGESTED ANSWER

It is generally accepted that rationing in the NHS is essential. It is simply not possible to provide every patient with every medication they could need. There must therefore be some rationing. Some people will not be able to receive all the medical resources they wish. Within the NHS, rationing occurs at a number of different levels. First, there is the decision by the Government to set the tax levels. Second, the Government determines how the tax income is to be distributed between the different departments. The Primary Care Trusts are then allocated their budgets. They must then determine policies to adopt towards the treatment of particular conditions. Finally there is a role for physicians in determining which patients are entitled to a particular treatment.[1]

The question for this essay is what role the courts should play when a challenge is made to a rationing decision. There are three ways that a challenge could be made to a rationing decision, although the most significant is judicial review.

The first claim is a breach of statutory duty. Under the **National Health Service Act 2006,** s 1 the Secretary of State is required to promote a comprehensive health service. That might appear to form the basis of a claim concerning a rationing service. However, in *R v Secretary of State for Social Services ex p Hincks* (1980)(considering the similarly worded **NHS Act 1977**) it was found that the duty was only to provide such services as he considered necessary to meet the 'reasonable requirements' as can be provided within the 'resources available'. It is therefore very unlikely that a Secretary of State will breach

---

1   In essays on rationing it is easy to forget that rationing occurs in different ways. The examiner will be pleased you are exploring the issues widely.

this duty. Indeed the **2006 Act** constantly uses references to what the Secretary of State considers necessary to meet all the reasonable requirements.

It is more likely that a claim could be made on the basis of judicial review of a decision by a PCT not to offer a particular kind of treatment. This is how most of the cases have come to court. The principles of judicial review apply, with most claims being that the decision was unreasonable or that there was procedural impropriety. There have been quite a number of cases now and the approach of the courts is becoming clearer. The following points emerge:[2]

1. The courts have accepted the principle of rationing. In other words, they have rejected an approach that says simply because a patient needs medicine the PCT must provide it. In *R v North and East Devon HA ex p Coughlan* (2000) the Court of Appeal accepted that the Secretary of State and PCTs have to operate within finite resources. Further, the courts have accepted that ultimately it is for the health authorities to determine how to allocate their health care resources. The Court of Appeal in *R v Cambridgeshire ex p B* (1995) acknowledged that in a judicial review the court will see the needy patient before them, but will not be aware of all of the other patients in the health authority's area. As the Court noted in that case, the health authority is in the best position to determine the best allocation of resources among all those in their area in need.

2. A rigid fixed policy is unlikely to be lawful. In *R v NW Lancashire HA ex p A, D, and G* (2000) a policy which said that gender reassignment was never funded was found to be unlawful as it was an improper fetter on the discretion of a local authority. There would be no objection to a policy which spoke about certain treatments generally not being available, as long as each case was considered separately. However, even there a health authority must tread carefully. In *R (Ross) v West Sussex Primary Care Trust* (2008), although the policy said that a medicine would be available only in exceptional circumstances, this was held to be unlawful because in fact the health authority simply refused all claims for medicine and did not have criteria against which to assess whether a case was exceptional.

3. If there is NHS guidance or NICE guidance on the provision of a treatment and a Trust wishes to depart from that guidance it must provide a good reason for why that should not be followed (*R v Derbyshire HA ex p Fisher* (1997)). In fact the NHS Constitution appears to guarantee treatment approved by NICE and so it may require exceptional circumstances for approved treatment to be refused.

4. The PCT, in deciding whether to refuse treatment in a particular case, must consider all the relevant medical evidence. In *R (Ross) v West Sussex Primary Care Trust* (2008) it was found that a medical report had not been properly considered by the body deciding to refuse treatment and so the decision was flawed.

....

2   Sometimes it is helpful to number points like this. If you feel this will make the point clearly then do it. However, your answer must be in the style of an essay, not a set of notes.

5.   If a patient is to be denied treatment they must be given the chance to explain why they should be given the treatment and to offer evidence. They must also be given reasons why they were refused treatment (*R v Ethical Committee of St Mary's Hospital ex p Harriott* (1988)).

6.   The courts will be particularly reluctant to overrule a clinical assessment that a particular treatment is in clinical terms inappropriate for a patient (*R v Secretary of State ex p Walker* (2000)).[3]

The overall picture appears to be that the courts seem to want to avoid being involved in the substance of the decision. They accept that the health authority is in the best position to determine how to allocate their limited resources among the very many claims that they have. What, however, the courts have insisted on is a fair and open procedure (*R (Otley) v Barking and Dagenham NHS* (2007)). The courts insist that decisions are made openly, and that criteria are set out and followed. There is much to be said in favour of this approach. It is almost impossible for a court to consider all the different calls on a health authority's expense and compare them. Even if a court had time to do that it is arguably a political question which should be decided by those responsible to the public, rather than the judiciary. The court plays the important role of requiring local health authorities to be open about what they are doing and the criteria that are used. As Keith Syrett has argued, it is important that decisions about rationing are made in an accountable and legitimate way.[4, 5] The approach of the courts plays an important role in achieving that goal.

If the courts were ever to change their stance the most likely route would be relying on the **Human Rights Act 1998**. A patient denied treatment might argue that a health authority denying treatment would infringe his or her rights under **Article 2** or **3** of the **European Convention on Human Rights (ECHR)**. Such claims are unlikely to succeed. Although they were relied on in the first instance in *R v Cambridgeshire ex p B* (1995), the Court of Appeal did not accept that a reasonable rationing decision could amount to an interference in **Article 2** rights. What might be more arguable is if a policy could be said to be discriminatory on the grounds of race, age or sex, for example. That might bring in **Article 14**. So far such a claim has not been the primary ground for challenge, but a case may appear in the future if there is blatant preference for, say, younger patients over older ones.[6] In *R(C) v Berkshire PCT* (2011) a transwoman seeking breast enhancement surgery failed in a claim that she was discriminated against because she was assessed using the same criteria for surgery that applied to women seeking such surgery generally. As she was treated like any other woman the court held there was no discrimination. It is likely that future cases will see more claims based on the discrimination ground.

....

3   This section has made good use of the case law, which the examiner will welcome.

4   Here you can show the examiner you have read some the leading writers in the field.

5   K. Syrett, 'NICE and Judicial Review: Enforcing "Accountability For Reasonableness" Through the Courts?', 16 *Medical Law Review*, 2008, 127.

6   The examiner will be pleased to see you looking to issues which might arise in court cases in the future.

Aim Higher ★
Explain carefully why the courts are not best placed to make rationing decisions. The point is that, although they can consider the case before them, they do not know about all the other patients who are calling on the health trust's money.

QUESTION 6
Critically assess the use of quality adjusted life years in rationing.

COMMENTARY
This essay is asking about the role played by quality adjusted life years in rationing decisions. Clearly in answering this you will need to start by explaining what quality adjusted life years are and explaining the role they currently play in rationing decisions.

How to Answer this Question
❖ Quality adjusted life years
❖ Difficulties in calculation
❖ Discrimination against older people
❖ Individualistic assessment
❖ Life-saving remedies.

Answer Structure

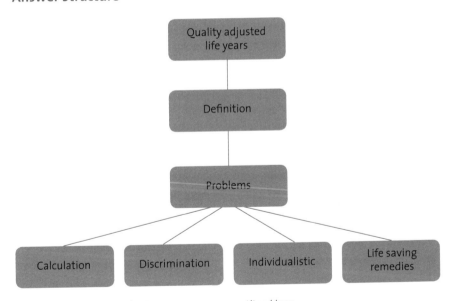

The main issues to consider in your answer are outlined here.

SUGGESTED ANSWER -

Quality adjusted life years (QALY)[7] is probably the most popular way of analysing the cost-effectiveness of treatments and is widely used in decision-making over rationing. It is used by the highly respected National Institute for Health and Clinical Excellence (NICE) and therefore plays a central role in the rationing of health care in the UK. In making a QALY calculation three factors are considered: the extra years of life offered by the treatment; the quality of those extra years of life; and the expense of the treatment. In short, it requires an assessment of how many years of extra life a treatment will provide, the quality of that life and at what cost. It would favour a treatment which would provide a patient with a year of good-quality life over one that would provide a patient with two years of low-quality life. The cost is crucial: a treatment which provides a large number of QALYs for a small amount of money would be highly favoured, while one which produced only a low number of QALYs for a large sum would not.

The QALY approach provides a way of deciding which treatment to choose when it might otherwise be hard to know whether the PCT should spend money on expensive cancer drugs or treatment. It can compare how many quality adjusted life years are produced for the money. Professor Sir Michael Rawlins, chair of NICE, suggested in 2002 that NICE would not support the funding of treatment over £30,000 per quality adjusted life year unless there were particularly good reasons to do so.[8] The Government, by contrast, have preferred not to use a precise figure. It seems that NICE still use the £30,000 figure even though it was first fixed nearly a decade ago.

It might be thought that QALY would be universally supported; surely it is sensible to use limited resources which create the most benefit. However, in fact, it has proved a controversial approach to use. We shall now critically consider some of the objections to it.

First, it is said that the calculation is simply impossible to use. How can one person assess the quality of a person's life? How can we compare an effective treatment for depression and an effective treatment for kidney stones? Trying to put a 'number' on different kinds of disease and calculate how awful they will be is simply impossible. The issue is all the more difficult because a particular condition will impact different people very differently. Arthritis affecting movement in the fingers might have little impact for some, but would cause major disruption for a professional musician. Either we need to assess the impact on each individual, which is complex and time-consuming, or we use generalisations, which might be unfair to people who are particularly impacted by some conditions. In response to these points supporters of QALY accept that these decisions are difficult, but that does not mean that an approach based on QALY should be rejected. Such issues are difficult under any approach. This response has much force. It is difficult to compare the

---

7   If you are going to use a phrase frequently it is fine to abbreviate it, as we did here, as long as you make it clear what the abbreviation stands for.

8   Here the answer is being precise, by referring to the chair of NICE by name and the exact figure used.

impact of different diseases, but that seems inevitable if there is to be rationing of medical treatment.

Second, it is said that it produces results that are unacceptable. Schlander (2008)[9] argues that a QALY approach would support the use of medication for erectile dysfunction but not treatment for multiple sclerosis.[10] That is because the medication for erectile dysfunction is very effective, while the treatment for multiple sclerosis assists with the symptoms of MS but still leaves the individual facing many difficulties. He argues that such a result is unacceptable. We should prefer treatments for those with serious diseases if it slightly alleviates their condition over treatments for people who are generally well. Supporters of QALY argue that such arguments play on our natural sympathy for those with serious conditions. While we naturally feel sorry for them, giving them expensive medication which has little impact on their lives is not cost-effective.

A third concern, and this is perhaps one of the most serious challenges to QALY, is that it is ageist. The simple point is that an older person would find it much harder than a young person to show that there will be a significant number of QALYs ahead of them. To take a simple case, imagine there are two candidates for a kidney. One is 20 and the other 70. If you asked how many years each would benefit from the kidney, the 20-year-old would be bound to win. Similarly, if you were looking at funding medicine that was used primarily by older patients or medication used primarily by younger patients, the latter would score more highly in QALY. The same point could be made about those who are suffering terminal illnesses. They will likewise struggle to show that they will gain many QALYs. Supporters of QALY might respond that such an approach is entirely justified. A person is not being discriminated against because of their age; it is just that the treatment has less benefit for them than it does for others. This is not, therefore, age discrimination. Or even if it is, it is justified because the NHS is entitled to ensure that it gets the most benefit from the treatments it offers. John Harris responds to this by arguing that we should be treating people as individuals.[11] All patients who will benefit from a treatment should be treated equally. We should not start preferring the younger or healthier of that group. Doing so infringes a basic legal and moral requirement of justice. Harris would make the point that treating younger and older patients differently in this context is, in effect, valuing some people's lives less than others. Harris says that if there is a fire in a theatre it would not be acceptable to allow younger people out before older people. Similarly, we should not do the equivalent in rationing treatment. Supporters of QALY would repeat their argument that they are not seeking to judge the value of people's lives, but rather the good achieved by treatments. This is a fundamental issue of disagreement between supporters and opponents of QALY. For an individual patient denied treatment in

....

9   There is a helpful reference here to one of the leading articles in the area.

10   M. Schlander, 'The use of cost-effectiveness by the National Institute for Health and Clinical Excellence (NICE): no(t yet an) exemplar of a deliberative process', 34 *Journal of Medical Ethics*, 2008, 534.

11   J Harris, 'It's not NICE to discriminate', 31 *Journal of Medical Ethics*, 2005, 373.

preference to a younger patient it is difficult to avoid the perception that one's life has been regarded as less valuable (see Quigley 2007[12]). However, from the point of view of an NHS manager it is easy to see how this can be regarded as a sensible use of economic resources (see Claxton and Culyer[13]). This is not an easy issue. The difficulty with rationing is that inevitably it can be seen as judging the value of people's lives and perhaps we need to be more open about that. Indeed, the fact that we find it so discomfiting produces a strong case for ensuring that there is sufficient funding for the NHS to ensure that we have to consider it as rarely as possible.[14]

The point just made feeds into another issue, and that is whether account should be taken of the broader circumstances of the illness. Should a patient who is at fault in being ill (e.g. they are a smoker) be placed further down the list than a patient who is blameless? Or should a person who is playing an important role in society (e.g. they are a research scientist) be preferred over a person who is not (e.g. they are unemployed)? QALY would not take into account the cause of the illness, but some commentators think that is misguided. NICE has said that a person's background or the cause of their condition should not be taken into account, unless it will impact on the potential effectiveness of their treatment. This seems the correct approach because it is difficult to determine the extent to which a person is to be blamed for their condition. Smoking was used above as an example of where a person might be blamed for their condition, but smoking is strongly linked to socio-economic circumstances and so the issue is far from straightforward.

A final complaint about QALY is that this approach tends to focus just on the particular patient and to be individualistic. A proper assessment of the benefits of a treatment would involve looking not just at the benefit of the treatment to the patient, but also the benefits to their families and those who care for them. Herring has argued that in calculating the benefit of a treatment the benefits to carers should be included.[15] However, that argument has its difficulties. It might mean that a person with many friends and family members will more easily be able to claim QALYs than a person who is more of a loner.

To conclude, QALYs do provide a useful tool in making rationing decisions. It is inevitable that we will want to assess how much good a treatment does if we are deciding which treatments should be available on the NHS or which patient should receive the treatment. However, it should be treated with care and should not be applied in a rigid

12 M. Quigley, 'A NICE fallacy', 33 *Journal of Medical Ethics*, 2007, 465.
13 K. Claxton and A. Culyer, 'Not a NICE fallacy: a reply to Dr Quigley', 34 *Journal of Medical Ethics*, 2008, 598.
14 This paragraph has set out the arguments on both sides of the debate well and explained why people disagree.
15 J. Herring, 'Caregivers in Medical Law and Ethics', 25 *Journal of Contemporary Health Law and Policy*, 2008, 1.

way. It should not be used to deny treatment so that a patient is left without dignity. It must be used with a careful and broad understanding of what is beneficial or harmful in terms of treatment. And we should ensure that it does not contribute to ageist attitudes.[16]

> **Common Pitfalls**
> Do not exaggerate the argument that QALYs are ageist. Most treatments will only have a benefit for the near future, in which case the age of the patient will be of little relevance.

QUESTION 7

Albert, aged 75, has a rare form of cancer. An experimental drug is available but his PCT has a policy concerning that drug that states that it is only to be used in 'exceptional cases'. The PCT has never found a patient wanting this drug to be an 'exceptional case', and when asked what would be an exceptional case has replied that a patient who was very young would be seen as exceptional.

Mary has high cholesterol. A drug has been approved by NICE for her condition. Her doctor refuses to prescribe it to her because he says that her high cholesterol is due to her lifestyle choices.

Susan is a lone parent with six children. She needs a very expensive drug without which she will die. The PCT refuses to fund her treatment on the basis that they cannot afford any treatment which costs more than £200,000 per year, as this does.

▶ **Discuss the legal and ethical issues raised.**

COMMENTARY

This problem question raises a number of issues around rationing. Notice that the examiner has asked you to discuss the legal and ethical issues raised. This may be because there are fairly few cases on the issue. So you will need to discuss how an approach based on QALY might work and the objections to that. On the ethical discussion, refer to the reports produced by NICE because that will give you some concrete material upon which to base your answers.

How to Answer this Question

❖ Albert: is this policy a fiction?; age discrimination
❖ Mary: use of blame for condition; relevance of NICE approval
❖ Susan: significance of children.

---

16 The conclusion has brought together some of the key themes in the essay.

Applying the Law

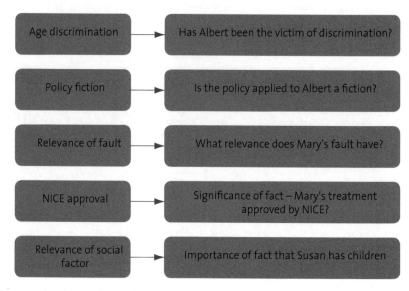

The main legal principles applied in this scenario are outlined here.

SUGGESTED ANSWER

Each of these cases will be considered separately and so we shall start with a discussion of Albert's case. Albert will have two main potential sources of legal challenge. The first will be by way of judicial review. He will not be able to argue that this rationing decision was *ultra vires* and one that the PCT was not permitted to make. It is well accepted that the health authorities are permitted to ration access to treatment, even if as a result a patient may die (*R v Cambridge HA ex p B* (1995)). However, Albert might claim that the health authority have improperly restricted their discretion. It is not permissible for a health authority to have a rigid policy denying treatment for a particular condition (*R v NW Lancashire HA ex p A, D and G* (2000)). Of course, the health authority will point to the fact that they have accepted that in exceptional cases the drug would be available. Albert could respond in two ways. One would be to refer to *R (Ross) v West Sussex Primary Care Trust* (2008) , where it was held that even though the Trust had said that in exceptional circumstances a drug would be available, in fact the Trust automatically refused all requests for it. In other words, the reference to 'exceptional circumstances' was really a fig leaf to disguise the fact that they were denying the drug to anyone. The court would look carefully at whether in this case the PCT had thought through what might be exceptional or whether it was a fiction.[17]

17   This essay has shown a good knowledge of the case law. Notice we have not simply listed the cases, but shown to the examiner we are aware of their significance.

We are told in this case that the PCT had imagined that being a young patient was exceptional. This might be open to challenge. The PCT as a public authority are required to act in accordance with the **European Convention on Human Rights(Human Rights Act 1998 s 6**). It is arguable that denying life-saving treatment interferes with a patient's right to life under **Art 2** or right to respect for private life under **Art 8**. More significantly, Albert can argue that they are doing so in a way which discriminates against age and so infringes **Art 14**. Although age is not mentioned in **Art 14** the list of prohibited grounds of discrimination is not closed and generally European law has been moving to outlaw ageism and prohibit age discrimination. It would be very surprising if it was not held that **Art 14**included a reference to age.[18] The health authority might reply that any discrimination was justified. It cannot provide treatment for all patients and so it must decide which treatments will offer the best value for money. It might argue that, given Albert's age and general health, even if the treatment is successful it would only provide him with a few more years of life. Compare that with a much younger person where a large number of years of benefit could be provided. It is difficult to predict how a court would respond to this issue. It might be argued that it is essentially a political question and the courts are not well placed to make an assessment of how resources should generally be provided for. Indeed, they may note that it is common for countries to use quality adjusted life years (QALYs), which do prefer younger patients over older patients. In that case Albert's case may fail on the basis that, although discriminatory, it is justified.

Turning to the ethical issues raised, the key one has already been highlighted. That is whether the use of QALYs in this case discriminates against Albert. John Harris has argued that it is a basic principle that all patients be treated equally.[19] So if the treatment is effective for Albert's condition he should not be treated differently from a younger person. Otherwise we are stating that Albert's life is worth less than someone else's (Quigley[20]). Rawlins has argued that what is being decided is the effectiveness of different treatments, not the value of lives, and so Harris' objection is misconceived.[21, 22]

Looking next at Mary's case, she will want to emphasise that under **s 8**of the **National Health Service Act 2006**the Department of Health has issued directions that PCTs should

18 The examiner will always be pleased to see sensible use of human rights arguments.

19 Harris, op. cit.

20 Quigley, op. cit.

21 M. Rawlins, 'National Institute for Clinical Excellence and its value judgments', 329 *British Medical Journal*, 2004, 224.

22 Although in answering problem questions the focus is normally on the case law, rather than academic writing, it is helpful to refer to the writing here as there is little case law.

provide treatments that have been approved by the National Institute for Health and Clinical Excellence (NICE). As the treatment in her case has been approved by NICE she could argue that it is unreasonable in the *Wednesbury* sense for a PCT to refuse her treatment. Indeed, one of the rights granted by the NHS Constitution is that patients are entitled to treatments and drugs approved by NICE. She may even be able to claim that the doctor refusing her treatment was negligent if she could show that there was no respectable body of medical opinion which would have supported her being denied the treatment (*Bolam v Friern HMC* (1957)). Of course the PCT in this case might claim that there was a good reason for departing from the NICE recommendation in that Mary has caused her own medical condition. That argument would seem weak, especially because the NICE guidance has made it clear that the fact that a condition is self-inflicted is not a reason for denying treatment. The doctor in this case would be on stronger ground if he had claimed that, as Mary would not change her lifestyle, giving her the drug would be ineffective, but that does not seem to be what he is saying.

The ethical issue centres on the extent to which a patient should have responsibilities for his or her health. Some commentators have urged for greater weight to be attached to the responsibilities of patients (see Brazier;[23] Herring and Foster[24]). However, such arguments in Mary's kind of case rest on an assumption that we know whether a patient has been negligent in causing their own illness. However, the extent to which a person is responsible for their own health and the extent to which it is fixed by socio-economic factors and the like, is highly complex.[25]

Susan's case raises some of the issues discussed in connection with Albert's.

As we have already said there, a health authority is entitled to refuse treatment on the grounds of cost even if without it a patient will die (*R v Cambridge HA ex p B* (1995)). However, the trust must have a flexible policy which involves considering each case separately (*R v NW Lancashire HA ex p A, D and G* (2000)). So if the trust has a blanket policy about drugs costing over a certain level then it may be that they have fettered their discretion and they will lose any claim Susan brings for a judicial review. Susan will seek to rely on the fact that she has many children to look after. However, that is a controversial claim. NICE in their guidance have said that a person's contribution to society should not put them in a more privileged position in relation to health care provision. That approach was accepted in *R (Condliff) v North Staffordshire PCT* (2011).

....

23 M. Brazier, 'Do no harm – Do patients have responsibilities too?', 65 *Cambridge Law Journal*, 2006, 397.

24 J. Herring and C. Foster, 'Blaming the patient: contributory negligence in medical malpractice litigation', 25 *Journal of Professional Negligence*, 2009, 76–90.

25 Here we are showing the examiner we are thinking of the long term problems that might arise if we start to blame patients for their health.

Perhaps her best argument would be, as Herring and Foster[26] have argued, that to assess the benefit of the treatment one needs to look at the impact of the treatment on all who will be affected, directly or indirectly. As six children are depending on her this will put her in an exceptional category of case and justify treatment. However, such an argument has proven controversial with Joanna Bridgeman arguing that we should not start to determine who does or does not have more people dependent upon them.[27, 28]

26 Herring and Foster, op. cit.

27 J. Bridgeman, 'Children with severe disabilities and their families: Re-examining private and public obligations from a caring perspective' in M. Freeman (ed.), *Law and Bioethics*, Oxford: Oxford University Press, 2008, pp 358–375.

28 Here a wide range of writing is being relied upon, which will impress the examiner.

Consent and Capacity

QUESTION 8

Assess the definition of capacity in the **Mental Capacity Act 2005**

COMMENTARY

This is student-friendly question. The examiner has been precise about what you are to discuss: the definition of capacity. It looks, at first sight, like a 'nice question'. Beware of two dangers.

First, the word 'assess'. That is not the same as 'describe'. You are not only to tell the examiner how the law defines capacity, but also you are to discuss it. Is it a good definition? What are its advantages and disadvantages? What problems will the courts have in applying it? An answer which simply described the law but did not analyse it would not score well.

Second, notice that the question is quite narrow. You are only asked about the definition of capacity. You will get no marks for talking about other aspects of the **Mental Capacity Act 2005** So keep focused on the issue asked. But think too about whether you have enough to say to answer this question. If the focus is on a narrow topic and it is one you have not revised much you will not be able to do well on the question.

How to Answer this Question

❖   The definition of capacity
❖   Issue-specific capacity
❖   The difference between capacity and wisdom!
❖   The dangers of prejudice
❖   The difficulties of borderline cases
❖   The ethical difficulties surrounding capacity.

Answer Structure

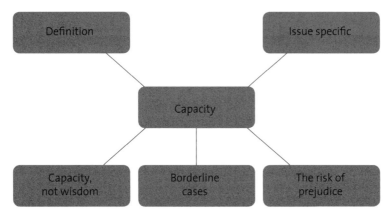

This mind map shows the issues around capacity to think of when forming your answer.

SUGGESTED ANSWER

Whether a patient has capacity or not is a fundamental issue in medical law. For if a patient has capacity then they have the absolute right to refuse treatment (*S v St George's NHS Trust* (1998)). If, however, a patient lacks capacity then a doctor can provide treatment which is in a patient's best interests. In this essay I set out the definition of capacity in the **Mental Capacity Act 2005** (**MCA**) and then look at some issues surrounding the definition.[1]

The **MCA** uses an issue-specific definition of capacity. This means that a patient (P) is not simply labelled as either having capacity or lacking capacity in general. Rather, it must be asked in relation to a particular issue whether P has the capacity to decide. So, a patient with severe learning difficulties might lack the capacity to consent to complex surgery, but certainly has the capacity to decide what they would like for tea.[2]

1   Use the introduction to set out the agenda for the essay.
2   Here we have used a practical example to illustrate the significance of the theoretical point.

The starting point for the law's approach to capacity is that a person is presumed to have capacity (**MCA, s 1(2)**). So if a doctor is uncertain whether or not a patient has capacity, they should be treated as if they do. The definition of capacity is found in **s 2(1)** of the **MCA** which states:

> A person lacks capacity in relation to a matter if at the material time he is unable to make a decision for himself in relation to the matter because of an impairment of, or a disturbance in the functioning of, the mind or brain.

Notably, the definition is restricted to cases where a person's inability to make a decision is due to an impairment in the functioning of the mind or brain. That clearly involves cases where a person has, for example, dementia or severe learning difficulties. The **MCA** Code of Practice explains that it could also include some whose brain functioning is impaired through alcohol or drug use. So a patient who refuses treatment due to their religious beliefs cannot be said to lack capacity as those beliefs will not affect the functioning of their brain.

A person lacks capacity if they are unable to make a decision for themselves. This is explained further in **s 3(1)**. It requires that a person be able to understand the information relevant to the decision; retain that information; use the information as part of the decision-making process and communicate that decision. As this indicates, there are a number of reasons why a person may lack the ability to make a decision for themselves. We will explore these next.

As **s 3(1)** makes clear a person must understand the information necessary to make the decision for themselves. However, that must be read in the light of other provisions in the **MCA**: **s 2** explains that all practical steps should be taken to ensure that a person is able to reach capacity. So a doctor cannot say a patient does not understand the procedure and so lacks capacity, if the patient would be able to understand it if the doctor explained it in simple terms. A doctor may even be required to use sign language or visual aids, if they will help a person understand.[3] This is important because it shows that the law prefers people to be able to make their own decisions. A person should only be treated as lacking capacity if it is not possible to render him or her capable of making their own decisions.

To have capacity a person does not need to understand all the information about their procedure. They need to understand 'in broad terms' the nature of the procedure (*Chatterson v Gerson* (1981)). So as long as they knew the central aspects of what the doctor was going to do there would be no need to understand all the issues. One controversial decision is *R v Tabassum* (2000) where a man, pretending to be medically qualified, gave women breast examinations. Although he touched them in exactly the

---

3   Here we show the examiner we are aware of the practical consequences of the law.

way a person doing a proper breast examination would have done it was found that they had not consented. They had not known of his sexual motivation and therefore had not consented.

A very important point to understand here is that the law focuses on whether a person understands the information.[4] They do not need to believe it. In *Re C (Adult: Refusal of Treatment)* (1994) a man was told by doctors that his foot was gangrenous and that an amputation was necessary. Without it, he was told, his life was in danger. The man understood what the doctors were saying and accepted that they were representing their views, but he believed that he was a world expert on foot disorders (he had a number of mental illnesses). He also believed that God would heal him. He refused to consent. Thorpe J held that he had capacity to refuse treatment. **He understood the relevant facts; it was simply that he disagreed with what the doctors recommended.** It is likely that a similar approach would be taken following the **MCA**. *Re C* could be contrasted with *R(N) v Dr M, A Health Authority Trust* (2002) where a patient refused medication because he thought the doctors were trying to change his sex. Here he failed to understand the treatment proposed by the doctors.

Not only must P understand the information, but they also need to be able to weigh it and make a decision. So if P is in such pain, or in such a panic, that they cannot use the information to make a decision then they will lack capacity (*Bolton Hospitals v O* (2003)). There have also been some cases where a patient has been under the influence of a relative or partner and so not able to make their own decision (*Re T* (1992); *Mr and Mrs A v A Local Authority* (2010)).[5]

An important principle underpinning the law is that P is not to be treated as lacking capacity merely because he or she makes an unwise decision (s 1(4)). There is always a temptation to decide that, because a patient has made a foolish decision, they therefore lack capacity. However, as we saw from the *Re C* case above, a patient may make a foolish decision and yet have capacity. That said, the fact that a patient makes a foolish decision can be evidence of a lack of capacity. Section 1(4) states that what is prohibited is deeming a patient incompetent 'merely because they lack capacity'. So their foolishness can be taken into account along with other evidence to find a lack of capacity.

Linked to the point just made is that **MCA s 2(3)** warns against assuming P lacks capacity merely based on their age, appearance or their behaviour. So simply because a person is singing manically or looks unkempt does not mean that they lack capacity. However, notably the Act uses the word 'merely' again. This suggests that if there are other factors that also suggest a lack of capacity a person's age or appearance or behaviour can be relied upon.

....

4   It is helpful to highlight to the examiner those issues you think are of especial significance.
5   Case law is used here to illustrate the points made.

Having set out the main principles of the definition of consent in the **MCA** I will now consider whether the test is appropriate. Any analysis of the test for capacity should start with a discussion of why the law thinks capacity is important. The reason is the weight that medical law attaches to the principle of autonomy. That is the principle that each person should be able to decide for themselves what treatment they wish or do not wish to receive. That involves a rejection of paternalism: the concept that doctors should decide for patients what is best for them. Instead autonomy says that patients should decide for themselves. Indeed their decision should be respected even though other people might think that decision foolish.

We can see in the **MCA**'s definition of capacity a respect for the principle of autonomy. We assume that P has capacity; P must be helped to gain capacity if at all possible; P must not be thought to lack capacity because their decision is regarded as foolish. All of these aspects of the Act reflect the principle of autonomy. However, there are two issues of difficulty.[6]

First, autonomy involves respect for decisions which reflect the thought-out views of a patient. Some philosophers argue that a decision which is illogical or based on false information should not be respected on the basis of autonomy. Indeed, a person's goals in their life might be frustrated if their misguided views are followed. Imagine, for example, a patient who wants to have good health but is terrified of needles and therefore refuses to agree to an injection. It can be difficult to know what it means to respect autonomy: do we follow his wish not to have an injection or his wish to have good health? As that example shows, it is far from straightforward what it means to respect autonomy.

Second, there is a difficulty in the law for those on the borderline of mental capacity. The current law could be criticised on the basis that it assumes that there are only two options: either a person has capacity or a person lacks capacity. This might be problematic in cases where a person is just found to have capacity, but wants to make a decision which will cause him serious harm. It might be argued (see e.g. Herring 2008[7]) that we need to have a category of those of borderline capacity where their views will be respected, but not if doing so will cause them serious harm. Others have argued that if a patient is making a decision which will cause serious harm, then the law requires a higher level of capacity than would normally be required (Buller, 2001[8]).

To conclude, we have seen that the **MCA** has provided a reasonably straightforward test for capacity. It seeks to promote the principle of autonomy: that where they are able to do

....

6   It would be an error to assume that autonomy is unproblematic. Here we show the examiner we are aware of the debates over autonomy.

7   J. Herring, 'Entering the Fog: On the Borderlines of Mental Capacity', 83 *Indiana Law Journal*, 2008, 1620.

8   T. Buller, 'Competency and Risk-relativity', 15 *Bioethics*, 2001, 93.

so, patients should make decisions for themselves. But that is only appropriate where the patient understands the key relevant facts and is able to use those to make a decision. The Act shows its support for autonomy by requiring decision-makers to ensure that patients are helped to achieve capacity where possible. There are some areas of concern, especially people who are on the borderlines of capacity. However, overall the Act does a good job of defining capacity.

QUESTION 9

Barbara has severe dementia and lives in a care home. She has little understanding of what is going on around her. Throughout her life she was a keen vegetarian. However, recently she has been seen taking meat from other patients' plates and eating it with relish. Her relatives (who share her vegetarian beliefs) have asked the care home staff to stop her eating meat.

▶ Discuss the legal issues raised.

COMMENTARY

This problem question involves discussion of Barbara. You should start by considering whether she has the capacity to make the relevant decision. This is key. Until you have resolved this issue you cannot properly start a discussion of the legal issues raised. If you think the answer to the capacity question is not obvious you should explain what the position will be if the patient has capacity and what the position would be if the patient lacks capacity.

If the patient has capacity the law is straightforward: they have the right to refuse treatment and to act as they wish. However, a patient does not have a right to demand a particular kind of treatment.

If the patient lacks capacity then the best interests test must be applied. That is not as straightforward as it seems! You will need to discuss carefully the different issues which a court will take into account in deciding what is in a patient's best interests. There is not a lot of case law interpreting the MCA to date, but use that which is available.

How to Answer this Question

❖ Does Barbara have capacity?

❖ If not, the best interests tests must be considered. Consider the weight attached to Barbara's current views; her past views; and those of her relatives.

Applying the Law

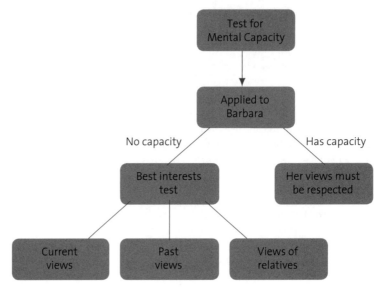

The implications of the Mental Capacity test in Barbara's situation are shown here.

SUGGESTED ANSWER

The first issue for Barbara is whether or not she has capacity.[9] The definition of capacity in the **Mental Capacity Act 2005** is issue-specific. So the question is not whether Barbara generally speaking has capacity, but whether she has capacity to understand the issues surrounding food. The definition of capacity is found in **s 2(1)** of the **MCA** which states:

> A person lacks capacity in relation to a matter if at the material time he is unable to make a decision for himself in relation to the matter because of an impairment of, or a disturbance in the functioning of, the mind or brain.

So how does that apply here? The answer is not obvious. On the one hand it may be said that choosing what one likes to eat requires only an ability to know what food one likes and Barbara seems to have that. However, it might be argued that her dementia means that she does not understand the ethical issues involved in eating meat. It should be added that a patient should not be treated as lacking capacity because other people think them foolish (**s 1(4)**). The **MCA** Code of Practice suggests that if a patient makes a decision which is 'out of character' that might legitimately lead to concerns that the person lacks capacity. It is difficult to know what a court might decide on this issue. It may be that

9   Here we have started with the key issue: Barbara's capacity.

s 1(2) MCA therefore plays a crucial role because it states that a person is presumed to have capacity. That means that if we are unsure whether Barbara has capacity to decide whether to eat meat we should assume she has. Given the uncertainty over whether she has capacity I will consider separately the legal position if she does have capacity and the position if she does not.[10]

If Barbara has capacity then her right to autonomy must be respected. That does not mean she has a right to receive the food she wishes. But it does mean she must not be forced to eat food she does not want to eat (*S v St George's NHS Trust* (1998)). So, if Barbara is found to have capacity the staff at the care home cannot be required to feed her vegetarian food. Nor can they stop her eating meat. However, they cannot be required to give Barbara meat unless doing so is necessary in her best interests (e.g. if it is the only food she eats).

If Barbara is found to lack capacity then she must be treated in accordance with her best interests. As Munby J emphasised in *Re MM* (2007) the focus must be on the best interest of the individual, in the widest sense including ethical, social, moral and emotional considerations. **Section 4** lists a number of factors to be taken into account in ascertaining best interests and these will be considered now.[11]

First of all **s 4(3)** states that Barbara's current wishes must be taken into account. However, they must be taken into account in so far as they inform an assessment of best interests. Unfortunately there is a dispute between judges on the correct interpretation. In *Re S and S* (Case 11475121, 25 November 2008), HHJ Marshall QC stated that the views of the person lacking capacity should carry 'great weight' in assessing a person's best interests. However, in *Re P* (2009) HHJ Lewison thought that was an overstatement. Academics have supported the view in *Re S and S* with Mary Donnelly[12] arguing that the views of a person lacking capacity should be followed unless there is strong evidence that acting otherwise is very much in their best interests. The argument the other way is that if a person lacks capacity their views are not the product of careful thought and so should not carry weight.

Second, the court will consider a person's past wishes and feelings and also 'the beliefs and values that would be likely to influence his decision if he had capacity'. In *Re G(TJ)* (2010) it was explained that this could mean that a decision which was altruistic could be made on behalf of a person lacking capacity, if when they had capacity they had been

---

10 Because it is unclear if Barbara has capacity, a good answer will consider the legal response if she has capacity and if she does not.
11 Here and in the next paragraphs we are showing a good knowledge of the detailed provisions of the statute.
12 M. Donnelly, 'Best interests, patient participation and the **Mental Capacity Act 2005**', 17 *Medical Law Review*, 2009, 1.

selfless. In this case weight will be placed on Barbara's prior commitment to vegetarianism. Her relatives may refer to *Ahsan v University Hospitals Leicester* (2006) , where a devout Muslim woman was involved in a serious road traffic accident and lost awareness of what was happening to her. Hegarty J held that it was in her best interests to be treated in accordance with Muslim tradition, even though she would not be aware of her treatment. It might be argued that the same should apply here. However, Barbara's case is different because she, unlike Ms Ahsan, has a current desire to eat meat. In reply it might be said that we should attach greater weight to Barbara's previous thought-out views than her current views, which are not the product of rational thought.[13]

Third, the views of Barbara's carers can be taken into account. Interestingly, s 3 does not refer to relatives, but rather those 'caring for' P and any person 'interested in his welfare'. In this problem question only the relatives are referred to but they are likely to be included under either category. Notably their views will only be of assistance in so far as they inform the court of what Barbara's best interests are. So the fact they will be distressed by seeing Barbara eat meat is not relevant, but their views on what Barbara would have wanted will be. Although, if they can show that their distress might impact on Barbara's welfare (e.g. if they were to visit her less) that could be taken into account Re Y (Mental Patients: Bone Marrow Donation) (1997)).

Another important issue here is s 1(6) of the MCA :

> Before the act is done, or decision is made, regard must be had as to whether the purpose for which it is needed can be effectively achieved in a way that is less restrictive of the person's rights and freedom and action.

This is significant in this case. If force is required to prevent her eating meat then it must be questioned whether that is really necessary. Section 6 requires that it must be a proportionate response, bearing in mind the likelihood of harm and the seriousness of harm. There is a code of practice that applies where force or restraint is to be used against a person who lacks capacity. That demonstrates that the use of force must be necessary. It seems unlikely in this case that the harm will be sufficient.[14]

All in all it is difficult to determine how the courts will determine Barbara's best interests in this case. It is suggested that, given the difficulties in preventing Barbara's access to meat and the reluctance the MCA has towards restraining patients, it is likely the court will not require the care home workers to prevent Barbara accessing meat.

13 The case law is used here to illustrate the application of the statutory provisions.
14 Here we are showing a detailed understanding of the working of the legislation.

> **Common Pitfalls**
>
> It is easy to assume that because a patient makes a foolish decision, they therefore lack capacity. However, the Act prohibits that line of thought. Of course the fact they make a foolish decision can be used in conjunction with other evidence to lead to a finding of no capacity.

QUESTION 10

Rowan used to belong to a small religious cult which opposed the use of vegetable products in medical treatment. Twenty years ago, he signed an advance decision stating that if he were to lose capacity he refused all treatment involving the use of vegetable products. A year ago he married and had children and stopped attending meetings of the cult. He has developed a rare, highly painful medical condition and has lost capacity. The only treatment involved uses vegetable products. Discuss whether it would be lawful for the medical team to treat him.

COMMENTARY

This problem question focuses on the advance decisions. It is a fairly small topic. If you have revised it you will be able to write a good answer. If, however, you have only covered it in outline, give it a miss.

One of the notable features of the **Mental Capacity Act 2005** 's treatment of advance decisions is the number of hurdles that need to be jumped before it can be concluded that an advance decision is effective. Revise these carefully and you will have a good structure for dealing with problem questions.

I have included in the answer a brief discussion of the ethical debates on whether or not advance decisions should be given effect. Normally in a problem question the focus will be on the case law and statute, but where the law is in the early stages of development it can be useful to refer to some of the philosophical debates.

How to Answer this Question

- ❖ Has the advance decision been made?
- ❖ Does it apply to the treatment in question?
- ❖ Has he acted inconsistently with the advance decision? Here consider marriage, children and leaving the cult.
- ❖ Are there factors present which Rowan had not anticipated?
- ❖ Note the defence of reasonable belief for the doctors.
- ❖ Set out the position if the advance decision does not apply.

Answer Structure

SUGGESTED ANSWER

An advance decision is defined in **s 24** of the **Mental Capacity Act 2005 (MCA)**:

> 'Advance Decision' means a decision made by a person ('P'), after he has reached 18 and when he has capacity to do so, that if –
>
> (a) At a later time and in such circumstances he may specify, a specified treatment is proposed to be carried out or continued by a person providing health care for him, and
> (b) Specified treatment is not to be carried out or continued.

There are a number of requirements that need to be satisfied before it can be concluded that the advance decision is effective.[15] First, it must be shown that Rowan was over 18 and competent when he signed the decision. We will assume Rowan was over 18. We can also assume that he was competent. The fact that his decision might be regarded as unwise by some (**MCA, s 1(4)**) cannot alone be evidence that he lacked capacity.[16]

Second, an advance directive only comes into force when a patient lacks capacity. We are told that Rowan has lost capacity. This requirement is, therefore, satisfied.

Third, the advance decision is only effective in so far as it relates to refusals of treatment (**MCA, s 24**). It does not apply to requests for treatment (*R (Burke) v GMC* (2005)). In this case Rowan is refusing treatment and so this requirement is also satisfied.

---

15 The statutory provision is complex and so it is helpful to break it down into its component parts.
16 Here we are not only referring to the statute, but also explaining how it applies to the case at hand.

Fourth, the advance decision must not be withdrawn. This includes where the person has done something that is inconsistent with the advance decision. That will be relevant here because it might be argued that Rowan's leaving of the religious group means he is acting inconsistently with the decision. However, against that, it might be said that while leaving the group does not support the decision, it does not indicate that he rejects the decision. The court could refer to the case of *HE v A Hospital NHS Trust* (2003) (Fam), which was decided before the **MCA** was passed. In that case a patient signed an advance decision indicating that she did not want to be given a blood transfusion.[17] At the time she was a Jehovah's Witness. Several years later she was involved in a car accident and needed a blood transfusion. The court heard evidence that she was no longer an active Jehovah's Witness and, indeed, had become engaged to a Muslim. That was accepted as evidence that the advance decision did not need to be followed. As that case was heard before the **MCA** it is possible that the courts will take a stricter approach after the legislation. Notably in *HE v A Hospital NHS Trust* the court placed weight on the fact that if there was a question mark over the validity of an advance decision in a life or death case, the preference for life would be respected. That said, the **MCA** does not include such a presumption under the **MCA**. That does mean that the courts will not read one into the Act. However, it may well be that the court will be reluctant to allow Rowan to die on the basis of a document we can be fairly confident no longer represents his beliefs.

Fifth, the advance decision need not be enforceable if 'there are reasonable grounds for believing that circumstances exist which P did not anticipate at the time of the advance decision, and which would have affected his decision had he anticipated them' (**MCA, s 25(4)**). In this case it might be said that when Rowan issued his advance decision he would not have foreseen that he would lose his faith; that he would get married; that he would have children; or that he would be suffering a painful condition. If the court were persuaded that any of these facts had not been foreseen at the time Rowan made the advance directive, and that had he seen them he would not have issued the advance directive in the terms he did, then it need not be enforceable.[18]

As the treatment in question is a life-saving one, **s 25(5)** is relevant. That requires that the decision be explicit in saying that the decision is to be respected even if as a result he will die. It is not clear in this case whether the advance decision contains such an explicit statement. If it does not it may not be followed.

17 It is always a good idea to refer to cases that apply the statutory provision you are discussing.
18 Remember it is not enough just to state what the law is. You must, as in this paragraph, explain how it applies to the case you are discussing.

This is not a clear-cut case and the**MCA** gives little guidance as to how the provisions are to be interpreted. In particular it is unclear from the legislation whether the courts should presume that advance decisions should be followed, unless there is a clear case that they are ineffective, or whether the burden is on those who seek to rely on an advance decision that they are effective. To assist the courts it may be useful to discuss some of the ethical arguments concerning advance decisions which have been promoted.

For some, advance decisions should be regarded as *prima facie* binding. They maximise a person's control over their life by giving them the chance, when competent, to make decisions about how they would like to be treated when lacking capacity (see e.g. R. Dworkin (1993)[19]). If we are dealing with a person lacking capacity we should listen to their earlier decision expressed in the advance decision, rather than the views of a doctor about what is in the best interests of the patient.

Those who oppose advance decisions do so on a number of grounds. First, it is sometimes said that the person who issued the directive is not the same person who now lacks capacity; or at least they lack the moral authority to speak for the person who lacks capacity. The argument is that when a person loses capacity, they lose their distinctive mental persona, its values and principles. It can be as if another person is living in the body of the person. The views of the original person should not, therefore, be imposed on the current person (R. Dresser (2003)[20]). A second point that is sometimes made is that it is impossible for us to imagine what we will want if we lose capacity. No one knows, for example, exactly what it is like to suffer severe dementia. Therefore any advance decision will inevitably be made based on a lack of sound information. A final point is made by Dresser (2003), who argues that our primary responsibility to those who lack capacity is to show compassion and to promote their best interests. An advance decision can never justify acting in a way that harms people.

Some commentators have seen the merits of both sides of the argument and have argued for a middle view. Maclean (2008)[21] suggests that an advance decision should be followed unless it causes the patient serious harm. Herring (2009)[22] argues that it should be followed only if it does not cause harm.[23]

All in all, it seems there is in this instance a reasonably strong case for saying that the advance decision does not apply. It may well be found that by leaving the faith he has acted

....

19 R. Dworkin, *Life's Dominion*, London: Harper Collins, 1993.

20 R. Dresser, 'Precommitment: a misguided strategy for securing death with dignity' (2003) 81 *Texas Law Review*, 1823.

21 A. Maclean, 'Advance directives and the rocky waters of anticipatory decision-making', 17 *Medical Law Review*, 2008, 1.

22 J. Herring, 'Losing it? Losing what? The law and dementia', 21 *Child and Family Law Quarterly*, 2009, 3.

23 Here there is a helpful reference to some of the leading articles discussing the theoretical issues.

inconsistently with the directive. Further, a court may well find that he had not foreseen the circumstances which later arose. It should be added that s 26(2) MCA provides a defence to a person who is satisfied that a directive is not applicable, when in fact it is.

If the advance decision is not enforceable then the central issue is a matter of best interests. In this case it is in Rowan's best interests to receive the life-saving treatment. Only in extreme cases, such as those involving PVS (PVS stands for persistent vegetative state, which is a medical condition where the patient is in a permanent coma), have courts held that it may not be in a person's best interests to be kept alive.

> ### Aim Higher
> While the **MCA** has given greater effect to advance decision than the previous law, notice how many ways there are of deciding that the advance decision is not effective.

QUESTION 11

Does the current law on children's consent to medical treatment adequately protect their rights?

COMMENTARY

In order to determine whether the current law protects children's rights, you need to start by setting out what the law is. The law on children and consent is quite complex and you will need to show the examiner that you are clear on what the law is. There is also quite a bit of material to go through. You will need to make sure you don't get distracted by the detail of the law or you will run out of time. Sketching an outline of your answer should ensure that you are able to be aware of how you are progressing and whether you need to speed up!

Have a think before writing the essay what the examiner has in mind in asking this question. Why might it be thought that the law does not protect children's rights adequately? A key point to bring out is the difference the courts have drawn between cases where children have consented to be treated and where children are refusing treatment. While, arguably, the law has protected well the right to consent to treatment, it has not protected so well the right to refuse treatment. This is a key issue to discuss in this essay.

How to Answer this Question

- ❖ The current law on children's consent
- ❖ *Gillick* competent children
- ❖ Children who refuse treatment

❖   Children who consent to treatment
❖   Cases where the courts need to decide what should happen to children.

Answer Structure

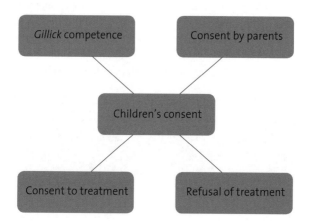

This mind map shows the issues around children's consent to think of when forming your answer.

SUGGESTED ANSWER

There are many who believe that the current law fails to protect the rights of children in the context of medical law. This essay will set out the current position, before considering whether or not children's rights are adequately protected. Before considering the issue further it should be emphasised that under s 1 Family Law Reform Act 1969, a child is a person under the age of 18.[24]

The starting point is that a doctor who treats a patient requires legal authorisation. For adults this comes, normally, from the consent of the patient. Without legal authorisation (or a flak jacket as Lord Donaldson put it in Re W (1992)) a doctor will be committing a tort or a crime. For a child the flak jacket (legal authorisation) can be provided in four ways:

(1)   The consent of a competent child or a child aged 16–17
(2)   The consent of a person with parental responsibility
(3)   An order of the court
(4)   The defence of necessity.

Each of these will be explained. Section 8 of the Family Law Reform Act 1969 explains that a child aged 16 or 17 can consent to medical treatment in the same way as an adult.

---

24 It is often helpful to start with a definition of some of the key terms used in the exam question asked.

Of course a 16- or 17-year-old may lack mental capacity (just as an adult might), in which case they will be dealt with under the **Mental Capacity Act 2005**.

In the decision of the House of Lords in *Gillick v W. Norfolk AHA* (1985) their lordships recognised that a child may be sufficiently mature to make decisions for himself. The case involved an application by Mrs Gillick for an order that contraceptive advice could not be provided to her daughters without her consent. She was defeated in the House of Lords where it was held that if the daughters were of sufficient maturity to understand the issue and their doctors decided it was in their interests, it was acceptable to give them the contraceptive advice and treatment. In order to be *Gillick* competent a child must have sufficient maturity and intelligence to understand fully what is proposed. The child has to understand what the treatment involves, the consequences of not having treatment and the effect of the treatment. So in *Re E* (1993), because the boy did not understand the way he would die, he lacked capacity to refuse a blood transfusion. Their lordships added that the child needs to understand not only the medical issues but also the moral and family issues. One issue the court will consider in particular is whether the child is simply repeating her parents' views or whether she is sufficiently mature to have her own views (*Re S* (1993)).[25]

A person with parental responsibility can also provide the doctor with a 'flak jacket'. Notably, not all fathers will have parental responsibility and some people will have parental responsibility even though they are not parents. Significantly, the law has developed so that a person with parental responsibility can consent to treatment even though the child is refusing to consent. That is so even where the child has *Gillick* competence. That was confirmed controversially in *Re R* (1991) and *Re W* (1992). The Court of Appeal explained there that although in *Gillick* their lordships had said that a competent child could consent, that did not mean that a competent child had the right to refuse. This approach was approved in *R (Axon) v Secretary of State for Health* (2006). There Silber J explained that a doctor could provide a child under the age of 16 with an abortion, even without the consent of a parent. Indeed he held that the doctors could carry out the termination without even informing the parents.

If neither the competent child nor the person with parental responsibility consents then doctors can make an order to approve treatment. That can be done under **s 8 Children Act 1989** or the inherent jurisdiction. The court will decide based on what is in the best interests of the child. The views of doctors and parents will be taken into account, but ultimately the court must decide overall what order will best promote the child's welfare (*NHS Trust v A* (2007)).[26]

---

25 Here the case law that has arisen after *Gillick* is used to explain the limitations on the doctrine developed in that case.

26 The case is used here to highlight the kind of factors the court will take into account when exercising its discretion.

Finally, doctors can rely on the defence of necessity. This is only available where a doctor needs to provide treatment to a child which will be in the best interests of the child (*Glass v UK* (2004)). If there is time for a doctor to go to court to seek authorisation then he or she must do so.

From the perspective of children's rights the current law might be criticised. On the one hand the decision in *Gillick* has been widely welcomed. It recognises that fixing the line between adulthood and childhood at age 16 is arbitrary. Some children under 16 are as mature as those over 16. Where a doctor decides that a child is as knowledgeable and mature as the average adult there does not seem to be a good reason not to allow the doctor to provide the treatment requested. While parents have rights and authority over children while they still need parents to make decisions on their behalf, in relation to a mature child the argument seems weaker.

What, however, may be criticised is the case law after *Gillick*, which stated that although a competent child could consent to treatment, if she refused then parents could consent on her behalf. However, the logic of the *Gillick* approach is that if a child is as mature as an adult she should be treated in the same way as an adult whether she is agreeing to treatment or refusing. As Bainham (1992) argues it, the law seems illogical.[27] It appears to say to a child: 'If you are mature we will treat you in the same way as an adult if you consent to treatment, but not if you refuse treatment.'[28]

However, to others the law has a certain logic. Lowe and Juss (1993) argue that the law is based on the principle that we want children to receive treatment which is in their best interests.[29] The law is engineered to make it as easy as possible for a doctor to provide the treatment a child needs. They can rely on the consent of either a competent child, or someone with parental responsibility or a court order. From this perspective *Gillick* is better regarded as a case where the courts did not want to allow Mrs Gillick to be able to veto the provision of beneficial treatment for her daughter, rather than a case about children's rights.

At the end of the day, then, the question is not whether the current law protects children's rights, but rather which rights of children we think need protecting. Is it more important to protect children from harm, or more important to allow mature children to make decisions for themselves? The law seems to take the view that we will allow children to make some decisions, but not where doing so will leave the child without treatment that they need. Perhaps what best justifies the current approach is that

....

27 A. Bainham, 'The Judge and the competent minor', 108 *Law Quarterly Review*, 1992, 194.

28 Where possible refer to specific academics who have written about the issues you are discussing.

29 N. Lowe and S. Juss, 'Medical treatment – pragmatism and the search for principle', 56 *Modern Law Review*, 1993, 865.

allowing a child to refuse life-saving treatment will deny them autonomy at any point in the future. If we have a niggling doubt that under-16-year-olds could be as competent as an adult it means we prefer letting them live to fight another day.[30]

Common Pitfalls

Do not assume that every parent has parental responsibility. An unmarried father who is not registered on the birth certificate of his child will not have parental responsibility for the child.

---

30 This conclusion brings together the threads of the essay well.

Confidentiality

4

QUESTION 12

Discuss the different sources of the legal right to medical confidentiality.

COMMENTARY

One of the striking features of the law on medical confidentiality is that a legal claim can be made on quite a number of different bases. This essay question is asking you to set out what they are and then to discuss them.

When considering the alternative legal sources of the claim there are two main issues to discuss. The first is: what are the criteria that need to be satisfied before the claim can be made? You will want to tell the examiner in what kinds of cases, for example, a contract claim would not be appropriate and when the case is more suited to a claim in tort. The second is to explain the differences in the remedies that the different jurisdictions offer.

A really good answer will go a bit deeper and explain how the different sources of the right reflect different reasons for why a breach of confidentiality might be wrong. Although the range of jurisdictions is often criticised for being confusing, its benefit is that it explains the various reasons for why medical information should be kept confidential.

How to Answer this Question

- ❖ Set out the range of sources for liability for breach of medical confidence:
  - ❖ Contract law
  - ❖ Tort law
  - ❖ Equity
  - ❖ Human rights
  - ❖ Statute
  - ❖ Criminal law
  - ❖ Professional bodies.
- ❖ Consider the differences in the criteria that need to be established and the different remedies available.
- ❖ Explain how the different sources reflect different reasons.

Answer Structure

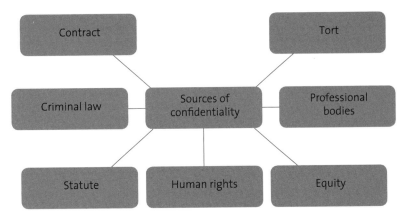

This mind map shows the issues around sources of confidentiality that should be discussed in your answer.

SUGGESTED ANSWER

It is widely accepted that if a doctor or other medical professional receives confidential medical information about a patient they must keep that secret. That basic obligation goes back to the Hippocratic Oath. It is not surprising that the obligation is found in law too.[1] As the title to this essay suggests there are, in fact, a variety of legal claims that could be made. These are appropriate in different kinds of cases and can include different remedies. This essay will set these out and explain the differences. It will also seek to

---

1 Here you are showing the examiner you are aware that there is a crucial difference between the ethical obligations a doctor has and the legal ones.

show how this confusing array of remedies simply reflects the fact that protection of medical confidentiality can be justified in a number of ways.

One source of a legal claim could be breach of contract. Disclosing medical confidential information could be in breach of either an express or implied term of a contract. However, this remedy is far less extensive than might appear at first. That is because there is no contract between an NHS patient and NHS staff. So the only case where it would be appropriate is where a patient was receiving private treatment.[2] Even then there may be terms in the contract which restrict liability. Damages would seek to put the individual in the position they would have been in had the confidentiality been kept. So any financial loss that flowed from the breach could be recovered, but damages for hurt feelings would be limited. A medical professional who breaches confidentiality might also be breaching the health care professional's contract of employment. This might lead to a claim from their employer, but not the patient (*Swinney v CC of Northumbria Police* (1996)).

A claim in tort could be used, probably relying on the tort of negligence. There would be no need to show that there was a contract between the parties and so it could be used even in an NHS setting. The normal rules of negligence would apply; in particular the *Bolam* test would be used. So a professional would have a defence if they could show there was a respectable body of opinion that would have supported the disclosure of the information. That suggests that if the case is a borderline one, for example there was an arguable justification for breach, then it is unlikely that the case will succeed. The damages that are available are based on the normal tort basis: they put the claimant in the position as if the breach had not occurred. Again, this will mean that if there is no financial loss or physical injury flowing from the breach then damages will be limited.[3]

Another tort claim would be to rely on defamation. This would only apply if the information disclosed was untrue. It would also be needed to show that it caused reasonable people to think less of the patient. This means it is unlikely to be used in breach of medical confidentiality cases. Doctors can also rely on qualified privilege if they reasonably believe the statement to be true and that the disclosure is to a person with a legitimate interest. These restrictions mean it is unlikely that a claim will succeed.

Yet another tort claim would be to rely on a tort of privacy. The courts are still developing this tort (following *Campbell v MGN* (2004) and *Douglas v Hello!* (2007)). In *Mckennit v Ash* (2006) the Court of Appeal accepted that the breach of privacy tort could be used to

....

2   Generally there is no difference between patients receiving private treatment and treatment under the NHS. This is a rare example of a case where there is.

3   The examiner will be pleased to see you thinking through the difficulties of relying on the different causes of action.

protect medical confidentiality. It would need to be shown that the circumstances were such that the privacy of the patient could reasonably deserve protection. It seems likely that in the medical context this will easily be established.

The most commonly used action in breach of medical confidentiality cases is to rely on an equitable breach of confidence. There are four criteria that need to be satisfied before the information will be protected. The first is that the information must be of a personal or intimate nature. Lord Nicholls in *Campbell v MGN* suggested that it might be helpful to ask whether the circumstances were that the person providing the information had a reasonable expectation that the information was to be kept private. It is likely that nearly all medical information would fall into this category. It may be that some information which a health care professional received during a visit (e.g. that the patient was wearing a new coat) would not be regarded as private. Baroness Hale in *Campbell* suggested that it might be easier to justify the breach of confidentiality in relation to disclosure of a minor medical complaint (e.g. the patient had a cold) than a case involving more personal information. The second element that needs to be satisfied is that the circumstances of the disclosure be such that an obligation of confidence can be imposed. Notably, the courts now prefer this form of the test, rather than asking, as they used to, whether there was a confidential relationship between the parties. This second element would clearly be satisfied in the case of information disclosed by a patient to their doctor in a consultation. It would also apply to any medical professional who happened to come across a patient's medical notes. The circumstances would be such that an obligation of confidence could readily be assumed. Less clear would be a case where someone approached a doctor at a party or in the street and asked a medical question. It may be, especially if they have seen the patient previously as a doctor, that any disclosures would be protected. But it is arguable that discussions over a dinner table could not be regarded as giving rise to the protection of confidentiality. The third element is that it needs to be shown that someone will suffer as a result of the release of the information. In *R v Department of Health ex p Source Informatics Ltd* (2000) it was held that the release of anonymised medical evidence does not breach confidentiality of medical information because no one was harmed by the breach. However, it should be noted that even if no individual is harmed there may be a harm to the public interest that justifies protection (*AG v Guardian (No 2)* (1990)). Finally, there will only be a breach of confidence if another person sees it. This last factor marks a clear difference from a breach of negligence, where a defendant could act negligently in leaving private information in public view even if, in fact, no one sees it.

Breach of confidence could be regarded as a human rights issue and indeed it increasingly is. The protection of confidential information falls within **Art 8 of the European Convention on Human Rights**, which protects the right to respect for private life. **Article 8(2)** permits the breach of the rights in **Art 8(1)** 'if it is necessary in a democratic society' in the interests of 'national security, public safety or the economic well-being of the country for the prevention of disorder or crime, for the protection of health and morals, or for the protection of the rights and freedoms of others'. In *Z v Finland* (1998) it was accepted that the protection of personal data was covered by **Art 8** and this was important to the House of Lords in *Campbell v MGM*. Following the **Human Rights Act** the courts must develop the law to ensure that there is protection of the **Convention** right to protection of confidentiality rights. A claim can be brought against a public authority which infringed an individual's rights under **ss 7** and **8** of the **Human Rights Act**. The damages are said to be such as seem just and appropriate. So if an NHS hospital improperly disclosed confidential information damages could be recovered.[4]

There are some particular situations where statute imposes obligations to keep information confidential. The most important example is the **Data Protection Act 1998**, which imposes duties of confidentiality in relation to stored data. There are also obligations that can be imposed by professional bodies such as the British Medical Association, the General Medical Council and the Nursing Midwifery Council.[5] These set out the obligations of confidence that are imposed on their members. Breach of them leads to internal regulatory punishment, the ultimate sanction being suspension from practicing or being struck off. The NHS has its own code of confidentiality which applies to all NHS employees. Where the patient is not so concerned about receiving a remedy which wants the individual who has behaved wrongly to be punished then this may be the best source of claim.

Finally there are some circumstances in which a breach of confidence could amount to a criminal offence. Most notably there is the **Computer Misuse Act**, which makes it an offence to access a computer database one is unauthorised to access. The offence is committed even where an individual is permitted to access one part of a database but in fact accesses another (*R v Bow Street Metropolitan Stipendiary Magistrates ex p Government of the USA* (2000)).

As can be seen, there is a wide range of sources for the law on confidentiality. Indeed one might say the law is a confusing array of alternatives, suggesting that the law needs a more coherent approach. However, it may be better to regard the range of remedies as reflecting the variety of wrongs that are committed when someone breaches medical confidence. This can be seen as a wrong by virtue of breaching an express or implied agreement that the information should be kept secret (contract); that the professional is

---

4   Here we have shown a good knowledge of the human rights arguments.
5   The examiner will be pleased to see you are aware of the professional codes of practice. For medical professionals these are often regarded as the most authoritative source of guidance.

behaving below the standard expected of a professional (tort; professional regulation); that the professional is infringing the human rights of the patient (**Human Rights Act** claims); that the professional is breaching the protection the law wishes to give to confidential information (equity). As there are many different wrongs, these are reflected in the range of remedies available.

> **Common Pitfalls** ✗
> Don't make the mistake of thinking you can sue an NHS doctor for breach of contract. There is no contract between the NHS and patients, and so only tortious actions can be brought.

QUESTION 13

When is a breach of medical confidence justified in the law?

COMMENTARY

This is a fairly straightforward essay question if you have revised the topic. You will want to show the examiner that you are aware of the different circumstances in which a breach of confidence is justified. Although the question does not ask you about the ethical issues raised it is still worth briefly discussing them. That is because the law is rather uncertain in some respects and as the courts clarify the law they are likely to be guided by ethical considerations.

You will want to show a good knowledge of the case law and refer to the leading cases, but be aware that this is an area of the law that is in a state of flux. Increasingly the courts have been using the **European Convention on Human Rights** in their discussions of the law. It may be that this will play an increasingly important role as the law develops.

How to Answer this Question

- ❖ Denials that the information is confidential
- ❖ Consent
- ❖ Proper working of the hospital
- ❖ Threats of harm to others
- ❖ Assisting police
- ❖ Press freedom
- ❖ Best interests of the person lacking capacity
- ❖ Good faith
- ❖ Other public interest
- ❖ Ethical considerations.

Answer Structure

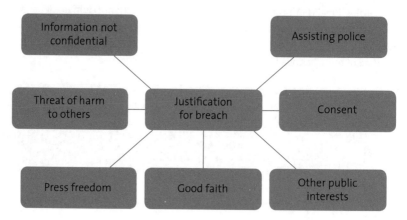

This mind map shows the issues around sources of jurisdiction of breach that should be discussed in your answer.

SUGGESTED ANSWER ------------------------------

In a claim for breach of confidentiality the claimant will seek to show that the information in question was protected by the law on confidence. If they are able to do this then the defendant will typically claim that the breach was justified. In this essay we will set out the circumstances in which the courts have recognised that a breach could be justified. Much of the law on confidentiality is shaped by the **European Convention on Human Rights (ECHR)** and so we will start with a consideration of that.[6]

Under **Art 8(1)** of the **ECHR** medical confidentiality is protected as part of the right to respect for private life. However, **Art 8(2)** allows an interference in **Art 8(1)** rights where it is necessary to do so in a democratic society in the interests of 'national security, public safety or the economic well-being of the country, for the prevention of disorder or crime, for the protection of health and morals, or for the protection of the rights and freedoms of others'. As we shall see, various exceptions to the law, listed below, can be explained on the basis of **Art 8(2)**. For now, a point to emphasise is that the breach has to be necessary in, for example, the interests of others. This suggests that it is not enough just to show that the breach is convenient but that it must be necessary.[7]

---

6   If there is particular part of your answer it may be best to start with that so you can show you are aware of its significance.

7   Always remember to explain that with rights under **Article 8** can be interfered with if the interference is justified under **Article 8(2)**.

One obvious defence for a defendant is to deny that the information is protected by confidence. It may be claimed that the information was too trivial to be protected by the law of confidence. Alternatively it may be argued that, although the information was at one time confidential, the actions of the patient have meant that it lost its confidential status. A good example of this is *Campbell v MGN* (2004). There the model Naomi Campbell was photographed leaving a meeting of Narcotics Anonymous. She claimed this breached her right to medical confidentiality. The defendant newspaper successfully argued that any confidentiality she had over her drug-taking had been lost because she herself had earlier made comments about her drug-taking. However, it was held she was still entitled to confidentiality about the treatment she was receiving and the details of it. This case shows that making public statements about a medical problem can mean one loses the protection of the law of confidentiality, but not automatically all protection.[8]

A less obvious way of denying that there has been a breach of confidentiality was shown in *R v Department of Health ex p Source Informatics Ltd* (2001). There GPs passed on anonymised information about patients to a drugs company. As the patients' information was removed the Court of Appeal held that there was no breach of confidence. There was no way that the drugs company could identify a particular patient from the information provided. This has proved a controversial approach to take. Jonathan Herring has argued that publishing a nude photograph of a person could still breach their privacy even if their face was obscured so they could not be identified.[9] Mason and Laurie point out that a patient may object to the use of their information even if anonymised.[10] A Roman Catholic may, for example, object to the use of their information to develop contraceptive treatment.[11] The response of the court of appeal to arguments like this was to deny that a patient could claim that the information was their property. Laurie has argued that, even if the information is not seen as property, it might still be intimate details connected to a person and so deserve protection.[12] But unless there is another decision of the courts it seems that anonymising the information so it cannot be linked to an individual patient may be a protection from a claim of breach of confidence.

The most common way of justifying a breach of confidence is to obtain the consent of the patient. This may be express or implied consent. If a patient agrees to be referred by their GP to a specialist they may not expressly say that they consent to the GP giving the specialist their medical details, but that can be implied. There may be some cases in which it is unclear to what extent a patient has given consent and as we shall see, the 'proper running of the hospital' defence may be more appropriate.

....

8   This case is well used as a vivid example of the argument being discussed.

9   J. Herring, *Medical Law and Ethics*, 3rd edn, Oxford: Oxford University Press, 2010.

10   K. Mason and G. Laurie, *Law and Medical Ethics*, Oxford: Oxford University Press, 2006.

11   This is a good concrete example, illustrating you are aware of the practical issues that can arise.

12   G. Laurie, *Genetic Privacy: A Challenge to Medico-Legal Norms*, Cambridge: Cambridge University Press, 2002.

It is generally accepted that in order for a hospital to run efficiently there needs to be a sharing of information between staff. It will, therefore, be a defence to an alleged breach of confidence that the breach was necessary for the proper working of a hospital (*R v Department of Health ex p Source Informatics*). A doctor may need to ask a nurse to administer medication; a specialist may want to discuss a case with a colleague. In cases like this it would be a huge administrative burden to obtain the consent of the patient every time. At one time the draft NHS constitution had a term that it could be assumed that patients consented to their information being available for research, but that was dropped. For that consent should be obtained. The defence could be justified on the basis that it is necessary to breach the patients' confidentiality rights under **Art 8(1)** in order to ensure efficiency of the NHS, which is in the interests of the state. This seems especially justifiable as most patients would readily consent to the disclosure.

Article 8(2) also justifies a breach where it is necessary to protect the interests of others. That can be seen in cases where there is a serious threat to others if there is not disclosure. The Department of Health refers to cases of murder, rape, child abuse or cases where there will be serious harm as justifying a breach. There is relatively little case law on the issue. The leading case is *W v Edgell* (1990), in which a doctor prepared a report for a patient who was being detained in a secure hospital. The doctor decided that the hospital had failed to appreciate how dangerous the patient was. He disclosed his report to the hospital, in breach of confidence. The Court of Appeal thought the risk he posed to others in the hospital if the report was not disclosed justified the breach. Bingham LJ held that the breach was justified because there was a real and serious risk of danger to the public. The risk was a real one and not a fanciful one. It was also emphasised that the doctor had kept the disclosure to the minimum necessary. Had he made the disclosure to the press, rather than the hospital and the Home Office, he may well have been found to be in breach of his duty.[13]

There is a tricky question where an individual poses risks to the public. In an American case, *Tarasoff v Regents of the University of California* (1976), a doctor treating a patient was told that he was going to kill his former girlfriend when she returned from her holidays. The doctor took no steps to warn the girlfriend and the patient indeed killed her. The doctor was told to owe the girlfriend a duty of care to take reasonable steps to protect her from danger. It is not clear that the same approach would be followed in English tort law because in England it is very rare for a person to be responsible for harms caused by a third party. In *Palmer v Tees HA* (2000) a health authority was caring for a man who killed a woman. It was held that they owed no duty of care because there was no way they could have known who he would kill, even though they were aware that there was a general risk he might be violent.

---

13 *Edgell* is discussed at some length here, but this is appropriate because it is such an important case.

A common reason for breach of confidence is if it is necessary to protect a child from abuse. Indeed, the GMC states that not only may a doctor make a disclosure in order to protect a child from abuse, the doctor must do so. In human rights terms there is a clash between the rights of the child to protection from abuse under either **Art 3** or **8** and the right of medical confidentiality under **Art 8**. Given that clash it is not surprising that the rights of the child win out.

Assisting police investigations is another justification for a breach. However, perhaps surprisingly, there are few circumstances in which a medical professional is required to disclose the fact that a patient has committed offence. One of the few is where there has been a road traffic offence (**Road Traffic Act 1988, s 172**). The Department of Health recommends disclosure where there is a grave offence (such as murder, rape or kidnap); or where no disclosure will seriously delay or prejudice the disclosure.

One of the most controversial issues is whether press freedom can justify the disclosure. A good example of the issue is *X v Y* (1988), in which two doctors were being treated for AIDS. A newspaper wanted to print the details of their cases to generate public debate. The court accepted that there needed to be a weighing of the public's interest in the debate and the principle that people's medical records should be kept confidential. They also took into account the fact that disclosure of medical records to the press should not be encouraged, and also that members of the NHS staff should be confident that they could seek medical treatment without fear that their medical records would be disclosed. In weighing up all the issues it was held that publication should not take place. One important factor was that there was already considerable debate in the press about medical practitioners with AIDS. Publishing the details of this case would not add much to the debate. In *H (A Healthcare Worker) v Associated Newspapers Ltd* (2002), which also involved health professionals who were HIV positive, the court saw the case as one involving a clash between the **Art 8** rights of the professionals and the **Art 10** rights of the press. The emphasis in the **ECHR** on the freedom of the press led the court to allow limited publicity about the case, but not involving disclosure of the names of the professionals involved.[14]

If a patient lacks capacity then it is permissible to disclose his or her medical records if that is in a person's best interests. So disclosure that assists in his or her care will be permitted, but not disclosure for amusement or the interests of others.

In *R v Department of Health ex p Source Informatics Ltd* (2000) the Court of Appeal suggested that there would not be a breach of confidence if the disclosure was in 'good faith'. This might well be questioned. In *Swinney v CC of Northumbria Police* (1996) it was

---

14 These cases illustrate well the difficulties with this area of the law.

emphasised that a breach of confidence did not require proof that the defendant acted in a deliberate way. From a human rights perspective the fact that the disclosure was in good faith does not justify an interference in a person's rights.

There is probably a catch-all defence that the disclosure was in the public interest. In *R v Crozier* (1990) a psychiatrist had prepared a report for a criminal case but due to an error the report had not been disclosed to the judge. He passed the report on to the judge and this was seen as justified in order to promote the proper working of the criminal justice system.

All in all, by way of overview we can see two main categories of justification for a breach of confidence. First, there are those which emphasise the autonomy of the patient. If the wrong of breach of confidence is seen as being an interference with the privacy or autonomy of the patient it makes sense that the consent of the patient justifies the breach. Second, justifications rely on the interests of others (e.g. cases of child abuse) or the public interest (e.g. press freedom). The difficulty for the law is that it is complex weighing up the interests of individual with the interests of society. It seems that where there is a strong state interest in this context it will be sufficient to outweigh the interests of the patient in confidentiality.[15]

> **Aim Higher**   ★
>
> Although it is normally not necessary to discuss overseas cases the *Tarasoff v Regents of the University of California* (1976) case raises an interesting issue. It is likely that English courts will refer to that case if they come to consider the issue.

QUESTION 14
Why should the law protect medical confidentiality?

COMMENTARY

This might seem a rather obvious question at first. After all, everyone agrees that medical information should be kept secret. However, the arguments for why this is so are not straightforward.

You could write an answer to this question which contains no law at all. That would not be a good idea. So you need to find a way to bring in a legal discussion. Remember that an answer with no law will never score a high mark. One way to tie this question into the

---

15 This conclusion brings together the main themes of the essay well.

law is to look at how some of the legal issues reflect the different views of why medical confidentiality should be protected.

You will need to think of a way of giving a structure to the arguments about confidentiality. A popular way is to divide the arguments up into those which are consequentialist and those which are deontological (see the essay for an explanation of these terms).

How to Answer this Question

- ❖ Consequentialist arguments in favour of confidentiality
- ❖ Deontological arguments in favour of confidentiality
- ❖ Arguments against confidentiality
- ❖ Why it matters.

Answer Structure

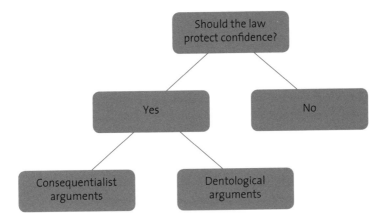

SUGGESTED ANSWER

There is widespread agreement that medical information should be kept confidential. However, there is less agreement as to why, or how strong those arguments are. The latter question is important because it indicates how easy it is, or difficult, to justify a breach.

In considering, firstly, the arguments in favour of confidentiality, these will be divided into those that are consequentialist (focusing on the harmful consequences if confidences are breached) and those which claim that deontological arguments are the key. These argue that there is basic wrong caused in breaching confidence which does not depend on the consequences.[16]

CONSEQUENTIALIST ARGUMENTS

There are said to be a number of beneficial consequences that flow from the protection of confidential information. The first is that patients will be completely honest with their doctors, disclosing all of their current symptoms and past medical history, without fear that the information will be passed on to others.[17] This has the benefit for the patient that they are likely to receive the best diagnoses and treatment. It has the benefit for the general public that the health service works efficiently and promotes public health. This argument is, therefore, that where confidentiality is broken not only is there a harm to the particular individual, there is also a wider harm to society because people will trust their doctors less and this will cause the problems just outlined.

These benefits are reflected in the law. They explain why the consent of the patient is a good reason for breaching confidence. Further, the fact that public goods, such as the effective running of the National Health Service, are seen as justifying breach suggests that it is similar public goods that are used to support confidentiality in the first place.

Not everyone is convinced by consequentialist claims relying on the public good of confidentiality. It is unlikely that a single breach of confidence will undermine trust in the medical profession. Further, it is not clear that it is the law that patients respect rather than the character of the medical professional they are dealing with. People have a strong incentive to be open about their medical condition in order to receive the best treatment. Confidentiality may, therefore, have a relatively small part to play in encouraging honesty from patients.

An alternative consequentialist argument is that patients suffer emotional distress if their confidence is breached. Going to a doctor requires the patient to become vulnerable and disclose information and their bodies to another person in a way they may not do with anyone else. If that vulnerability is misused by the doctor the patient may well feel manipulated and maltreated. This emotional harm, therefore, justifies the law on confidentiality.

This argument can only justify the law on confidentiality to a limited extent. Information may be disclosed about a patient, but the patient may never learn of it. They may even be

---

16 This is a helpful way to divide the arguments on this question. It also shows the examiner you are aware of the ethical arguments over consequentialism.

17 It is always good for a lawyer to show that developing the law requires rules that will achieve justice not just in the case at hand, but also in future cases.

dead. They may never discover the breach and therefore not suffer emotional harm. That does not mean that there is no breach of confidence. The psychological injury caused by a breach, therefore, is better seen as a factor which might make one breach more grave than another, but cannot explain the basis of breach of confidence.

DEONTOLOGICAL ARGUMENTS

These argue that there is a breach of a fundamental principle which occurs in a case of breach of confidence. Even if the patient does not suffer emotional distress and even if it is not possible to identify some harm to the public, to breach a confidence is wrong in itself. It is seen as part of the right to privacy. We need areas of our lives which we can keep private so that we can retreat to them to develop our own personality and character. Alfred Capron[18] talks of the need to respect reserve and solitude.[19] We must control the access to certain bits of information about ourselves to make life bearable. This is all part of the breach of autonomy: that a person should be free to decide how they wish to live their lives. This ties in with a range of other privacy concerns in our society such as the widespread use of CCTV cameras. Although it is hard to explain precisely what is lost when everyone about you is currently on view, we know that most people choose to restrict access to private information about themselves. The law recognises that through the law on confidentiality. To opponents of this approach this is all very vague. In truth, information about us is kept by a wide range of agencies. The notion that we readily keep secrets may have been true in the past but no longer.

A rather different deontological approach is to suggest that the wrong in a breach of confidence case is that there is breach of trust or fidelity. Again, these are wrongs, regardless of the consequences of them. This argument would not, however, explain why a person who has no relationship with the victim, but comes across secret information about them, is still required to maintain the confidence.

WHY IT MATTERS

As we have seen, there is a variety of arguments that can be used to support confidentiality. The best view is that it is a combination of the arguments used above that combine to produce a strong case in favour of confidentiality. The range of arguments explains why some breaches appear worse than others.[20] However, it is important to be clear on what the basis is in a particular case, for two reasons. First, it helps us define the principles to use for 'borderline cases'. For example, as already mentioned, if the wrong in breach of confidence lies in the breach of trust, then this will mean that a stranger is free to disclose the information, unless one of the other reasons

---

18 If you can, refer to specific authors in your essays.
19 A. Capron, 'Legal and ethical problems in decisions for death', 14 *Law and Medical Health Care*, 1986, 141.
20 It is always helpful to explain why what might appear to be very theoretical arguments have a practical significance.

is used to justify its application. Second, it helps us develop a coherent approach to justification for breach of confidence. If the wrong of breach of confidence lies in the harm to the public, then if we can identify a greater public good the breach may easily be justified. If, however, a breach of confidence is an interference in a basic human right then an appeal to a public good may be insufficient to justify the breach. Or at least there must be a significant public good if the breach is to be justified. So, although the arguments over the justification for the law on confidentiality may seem theoretical, they are in fact of considerable practical significance.

Aim Higher ★

Even with a question which is more theoretical, always bring the issue down to the ground by asking why the theoretical debates matter in practice. In what kind of cases does it matter which theoretical approach is taken?

Checklist ✔

You need to be aware of

- The legal status of the fetus
- The way the law regulates access to contraction
- The circumstances in which an abortion may be lawful
- The ethical debates over the status of the fetus and abortion
- The 'caesarean section' case law.
- The law on sterilisation of those lacking capacity

QUESTION 15

'The fetus has no rights or interests in law.' Discuss.

COMMENTARY

This question contains a quote which you are asked to discuss. Sometimes you are given the name of the author of the quote. If, as in this case you are not, you can assume that the examiner has made it up for the purpose of the exam. However, don't assume that because the examiner has made it up the examiner thinks it is correct. You need to decide whether the quote is correct or not.

Remember to focus on what is not asked as well as what is asked. Here you are asked to discuss the legal status of the fetus and whether it has any legal interests or rights. Notice that this does not require you to discuss what the legal status of the fetus should be, nor to discuss the moral status of the fetus. So keep focused primarily on what the current law is and turn away from the Sirens inviting you to enter the controversial moral issues!

It is understandable when thinking about the legal status of the fetus that candidates will think about abortion and that is quite proper. However, although abortion is an important area of the law it is not the only part that discusses fetuses. A good answer will deal with a range of legal arenas in which the fetus has been discussed.

How to Answer this Question

❖   Explain the issue to be addressed
  ❖ Does the fetus have rights in criminal law?
  ❖ Does the fetus have protected interests in the law on abortion?
  ❖ Does the fetus have rights under civil law?
  ❖ Conclusions about the legal status of the fetus.

Applying the Law

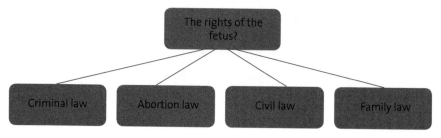

Branches of law that affect the rights of the fetus are shown here.

SUGGESTED ANSWER

The proper status of the fetus is one of the most controversial issues in medical ethics. However, in this question we have been asked to focus on the legal status of the fetus.[1] This essay will focus on the current law rather than enter the fevered territory of the ethicists. It will be noted from the outset that no consistent approach has been taken by the law towards the fetus. We shall examine how different areas of the law have treated the fetus, before attempting to summarise the status that it has.[2]

The first issue to examine is the criminal law. The fetus is not regarded as a person in the eyes of the criminal law. That is revealed by the fact that a fetus cannot be murdered. In *Attorney-General's Reference (No 3 of 1994) (1998)* a man stabbed his pregnant girlfriend, injuring the fetus. The fetus was born alive and the baby lived for over 100 days before dying from her wounds. The House of Lords confirmed that had the fetus died before being born there could not be a conviction for murder or manslaughter. However, as the fetus had been born and then become a person a manslaughter charge could lie.

---

1   Here we have shown that we have read the question carefully and are focusing on the specific issue asked.

2   The introduction sets out how the essay will address the question asked.

Similarly, in *R v Taite* a man who threatened to kill a fetus was held not to be guilty of the offence of threat to kill under the **Offences Against the Person Act 1861** because it was not a person. Another example of this is *Re J* (2006), where it was said that a pregnant woman could not be guilty of kidnapping a fetus when she left the country. So it is well established that a fetus is not a person in the eyes of the criminal law. However, that does not mean that the fetus is regarded as a nothing for the purposes of the criminal law. Indeed, such a view was expressly rejected by Lord Mustill in *Attorney-General's Reference (No 3 of 1994)*. He described the fetus as a unique organism. He explained that the fetus was not just a part of the mother, like a leg or an arm, nor was the fetus a nothing. As he explained, it was *sui generis* with some protections in the eye of the law. These can be found in the offences of procuring a miscarriage under **ss 58** and **59** of the **Offences Against the Person Act 1861** and the offence of child destruction in the **Infant Life (Preservation) Act 1929**. So, to conclude, for the criminal law the fetus is not a person, but is something that has interests which are protected by the law.[3]

The second issue to consider is abortion. The law on abortion is found in the **Abortion Act 1967**. It operates as a defence to actions that would otherwise be crimes under **ss 58** and **59** of the **Offences Against the Person Act 1861**. What does the Act tell us about the status of the fetus? One fact that is noticeable is that the Act does not simply permit abortion whenever the patient wants it or even whether the doctor or patient thinks the procedure is appropriate. One of the listed five grounds must be made out. This indicates that there is some public interest in restricting the procedure. It is difficult to see what this might be save some recognition of the interests of the fetus. Other medical procedures are not regulated in this way. Indeed the more advanced the pregnancy the more restrictive the grounds, indicating that the fetus's interests increase in significance as the age of the fetus increases. This is not, of course, to say that the fetus is recognised as having the same status as a person, but rather that the fetus has some interests.

The third question to consider is the civil law. Under the civil law a fetus is not a person until after birth. Only then can a child bring proceedings (or proceedings be brought on behalf of the child). So proceedings cannot be brought in the fetus's name to prevent an abortion, for example *Paton v BPAS* (1978). Similarly, if a fetus is injured pre-birth no proceedings can be brought unless the fetus is born alive; then it is a person with standing and can bring actions for injuries pre-birth (**Congenital Disabilities (Civil Liability) Act 1976**). This was explained in *Burton v Islington HA* (1993) in this way: the injury created a potential claim which crystallised at birth. This reflects the view that pre-birth the child is not a person. However, the law can recognise in some circumstances injuries done to fetuses.

3   This section has made ample reference to statute and case law to demonstrate a good level of knowledge.

Turning to family law issues. A fetus cannot be made a ward of court (*Re F (In Utero)* (1998)). A care order can be made in respect or a child immediately after birth, but not before. In part this is because the state or anyone else apart from the mother would not be able to care for a child *in utero*. In *Evans v Amicus* (2004) a man and woman separated and disagreed over what should happen to frozen fetuses that they had produced together. The Court of Appeal saw the issue as essentially a matter of interpreting the provisions of the **Human Fertilisation and Embryology Act 1990**. Although there was some discussion of the rights of the parties, Thorpe LJ stated that the fetus had no rights or interests under the law. He did not discuss the issue in detail and it may be he dismissed the argument too quickly in the light of the points raised in this essay.[4]

A final issue is the extent to which a fetus may claim a right under the **European Convention on Human Rights**. The leading case is *Vo v France* (2004), which involved a woman who, due to a medical mishap, had her pregnancy terminated without her consent (there were two Ms Vos in the hospital at the same time). There was no criminal offence under French law that was committed by the doctor. Ms Vo took the case to the European Court of Human Rights (ECtHR). The Court held that a fetus was not automatically protected by **Art 2** or **8**. Whether it was or not was a matter for the discretion of each individual country (within their margin of appreciation). In effect they dodged the question and now each country's own courts will need to resolve the issue.

So does the fetus have no intersts under the law? Not quite. The fetus is clearly not regarded as a person in the eyes of the law. However, there is some protection for the interests of the fetus. It is protected under criminal law and under tort law, providing the fetus later is born. The regulation of abortion likewise points to an acknowledgment of the fetus having some interests, but certainly not the same as those recognised as a person.[5]

> **Common Pitfalls**
> Students often look only at the law on abortion to ascertain the legal status of the fetus. Considering the civil law as well provides a broader focus.

QUESTION 16

To what extent would it be true to say that English law recognises a right to abortion?

COMMENTARY

In order to answer this question you will need to set out what a right to abortion means. What would a law which respected the right to abortion look like? Only when you have

---

4   Here there has been a good demonstration of a wide range of areas of law.

5   This conclusion provides a concise and measured summary of the current law.

determined that can you consider whether or not English law recognises a right to abortion.

It is important to put the **Abortion Act 1967** in its legal context. It amounts to a defence to what would otherwise be a criminal offence. Note also that the emphasis is on what the doctor believes. This counts far more than the views of the woman.

In order to determine whether or not there is a right to abortion you might want to consider how the law operates in practice. Indeed you will see in the suggested answer that the conclusion suggests that, although the law on the books does not suggest that there is a right to abortion, there is one, largely, in the way the law operates on the ground.

How to Answer this Question
- ❖ The meaning of a right to abortion
- ❖ The context of the **Abortion Act**
- ❖ The approach of the act
- ❖ The grounds for an abortion
- ❖ Abortion in practice
- ❖ Conclusion.

Answer Structure

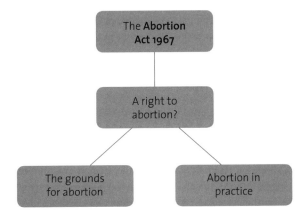

This mind map illustrates the main legislation and practical factors to consider in your answer.

SUGGESTED ANSWER

To start this essay I will outline what a right to abortion would be. When a person claims a right to X then this means that there is a duty on another person or the State to provide X. If the law protected the right to an abortion we would expect to see that there would be a duty on the NHS to provide abortion services. Further, that if a woman requested an abortion there would no further restrictions on access to an abortion. However, as we shall see, the actual law does not appear to match these criteria.[6]

The starting point for the law on abortion is that an abortion will be a crime, unless a defence can be found.[7] Under **ss 58** and **59** of the **Offences Against the Person Act 1861** it is an offence for a woman to procure her own miscarriage or for someone to supply an object for use in an abortion. The **Infant Life (Preservation) Act 1929** creates an offence of child destruction which is committed when a fetus over the age of 28 weeks is destroyed. The **Abortion Act 1967** and the defence of necessity can provide defences in certain circumstances, which we shall look at in a moment. Before doing so it is worth noticing that the fact that *prima facie* an abortion is a crime indicates that abortion is not regarded as a basic right in English law.

The **Abortion Act 1967** sets out the circumstances in which an abortion may be legal. However, there are restrictions on where the abortion can be carried out (in an NHS hospital or other approved place) and by whom (it must be under the authority of a registered medical practitioner). Most significantly, an abortion can only be carried out if two medical practitioners agree that one of the statutory grounds permitting abortion is applicable. It should be noted that the requirement of the Act is not that one of the grounds in fact applies, just that the doctors are of the opinion that it did. This means that an abortion will only be unlawful in cases where doctors are acting in bad faith when declaring that they believe the grounds to be made out. Notably greater weight is attached in the statute to the opinion of the doctors on whether one of the statutory grounds is applicable than on the opinion of the woman concerned. This makes it clear that abortion is not regarded as a right of the woman to demand when she wishes, but rather is subject to the control of professionals.

The grounds are as follows. The first applies only where the pregnancy is less than 24 weeks and 'the continuance of the pregnancy would involve risk, greater than if the pregnancy were terminated, of injury to the physical or mental health of the pregnant woman or any existing children of her family'. So the medical practitioners must be persuaded that there is a risk to the physical or mental health of the woman and that the risked harm is greater than would arise if the abortion were not carried out. It must be admitted that the terminology used here is vague. What counts as harm? Would it include emotional upset? There has been no guidance from the courts. It seems in practice that this is left to the doctors to interpret, meaning that a doctor who wishes to take a liberal approach will have no difficulty in finding that a woman seeking an abortion will suffer harm if it is denied. While a doctor who opposes liberal access to

6   The essay has started by explaining what a right means. The question cannot be answered until that task has been performed.

7   This is an important point to make in an essay on abortion.

abortion could take a much stricter approach and only allow abortion where there is a risk of very serious harm.[8]

The second ground is where the termination is necessary to prevent grave permanent injury to the physical or mental health of the pregnant woman. The third is that 'the continuance of the pregnancy would involve risk to the life of the pregnant woman, greater than if the pregnancy were terminated'. The very fact that these two grounds are spelled out indicates that the drafters were not imagining that there would be abortion on demand following abortion; rather they were imagining abortion being restricted to the most serious kinds of cases.

The final ground is that there is a substantial risk that if the child were born it would suffer from such physical or mental abnormalities as to be seriously handicapped. The last three grounds are available without time limit. In other words, even late abortions can be carried out on these grounds. Again they are restricted to the views of medical professionals rather than the woman's voice.[9]

Another notable feature of the **Abortion Act** is that under **section 4**, if a person has a moral objection to an abortion they are not legally required to participate in it. That too indicates that we are not dealing with a fundamental right or else the law would be stricter on when a conscientious objector would be required to assist. It could, for example, require involvement in an abortion if no one else was available, but the only exception to this is where the woman's life is in danger.

It is notable that, despite the apparently restrictive requirements for an abortion, there have not been any reported cases where there has been a successful attempt to restrict access to an abortion. In *Paton v Trustees of the BPAS* (1979) a husband failed to obtain an injunction to prevent a wife having an abortion without his consent. Sir George Baker explained that the **1967 Act** did not give a father a right to seek to prevent an abortion; indeed the Act did not even require his consent or notification before an abortion. This point was repeated in *C v S* (1988) where a man failed in his attempt to get an injunction to prevent his partner getting an abortion. Sir John Donaldson stated that even if there were suspicions that the abortion may be illegal, proceedings should be brought by the DPP or the Attorney General rather than a member of the public. Further, his attempts to bring proceedings in the name of the fetus were likely to be rejected. In *Jepson v CC of Mercia Police Constabulary* (2003) a curate was given leave to challenge the decision of the CPS not to prosecute a doctor who, relying on the serious disability ground, had conducted an abortion in relation to a fetus with a cleft lip. The CPS was ordered to reinvestigate the case, which they did, but they still concluded not to prosecute. The

8   There is no need to quote at length the precise statutory provisions. An accurate summary suffices.
9   The different time limits used in the **Abortion Act 1967** can be of great practical significance and so it is worth revising them carefully.

failure of these cases shows that the courts are very unwilling to police the operation of the **Abortion Act 1967**. That might suggest that, in practice, despite what the wording of the Act says, abortion is regarded by the courts as essentially a private matter between the pregnant woman and her doctor.

If we turn to abortion in practice it is interesting that over 90 per cent of abortions are performed under the NHS, although private establishments are regularly used. The s 1(1)(1) ground (risk to physical or mental health) is used in the vast majority of grounds (over 97 per cent). This has led some to suggest that doctors are very ready to accept that if a woman wants an abortion she would have one. Indeed, the fact that there have been around 200,000 abortions a year in recent years suggests there is not a huge barrier to abortion. There are, however, some reports of difficulties in access to services, and more presenting reports of long delays. Nevertheless, it is very rare to find a report of a woman who sought an abortion but was unable to find one. That suggests that in fact if a woman wants an abortion she is likely to get one, funded by the NHS.[10]

The issue of a right to abortion was considered by the European Court of Human Rights in *A, B and C v Ireland* (2010) where it was held that the **European Convention on Human Rights** did not automatically give a right to an abortion. It was a matter for each country to decide whether to give a right to abortion. That shows that if there is to be a right to an abortion in English law it must come from the national law and not European law.

In conclusion, if we look at the law we seem to be a long way from acknowledging abortion as a right. In fact it looks as if there is restrictive access to abortion and it seems that the issue is seen as a medical one. It is for doctors to determine whether there is to be an abortion; indeed the view of the woman seems to play little role in formal regulation. However, if we look at how the law works on the ground, although there are areas for concern, it seems nearly all women who seek an abortion on the NHS can have access to it, free of charge. That would seem to reflect an acceptance of a right to abortion.

Aim Higher ★

Bring in information about abortion in practice. It is important to look at the formal legal rules about abortion, but it is also important to consider how the provision of abortion works on the ground.

---

10   The examiner will be pleased to see you showing an awareness of how the law works in practice.

QUESTION 17

Mary was 16 weeks pregnant when she was involved in a serious car accident. She has been diagnosed as being in a permanent coma. Tom, her husband, wants her to be kept in a coma so that the pregnancy can be brought to term. Susan, Mary's sister, thinks that Mary will not benefit from being kept alive and therefore should be allowed to die. The medical team side with Susan, but Tom is bringing the case to court, seeking a declaration that Mary be placed on the ventilator. Assess what legal issues are raised.

COMMENTARY

The examiner has deliberately chosen a scenario which is yet to be considered in a reported case by the English courts. So don't worry if the answer is not obvious or you cannot think of a directly relevant case. You need to go back to first principles and think of different ways of looking at this case.

One obvious starting point is the **Mental Capacity Act 2005** and the best interests test. The other is to think whether the legal status of the fetus has a bearing on the approach to take. A third possibility is drawing an analogy with the **Abortion Act 1957**. There is no 'right' answer and it is a matter of considering which of these approaches is most likely to be adopted by the court.

How to Answer this Question

❖ **Mental Capacity Act**: application of best interests test
❖ The legal status of the fetus
❖ An analogy with abortion?

Applying the Law

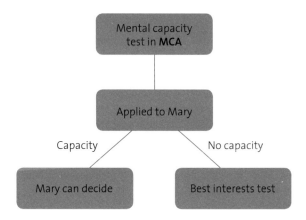

This diagram shows the implications of the mental capacity test in Mary's situation.

SUGGESTED ANSWER

There are a number of different ways that a court could address this issue. I will take these in turn.

As Mary is in a coma she clearly lacks capacity to make decisions for herself. Her treatment should therefore be governed by the **Mental Capacity Act 2005.** Section 4 explains that in relation to patients who lack capacity the test which governs how they should be treated is the best interests test. This can involve consideration of a wide range of issues. In this case the following may be considered.[11]

First, it was explained in the case of *Bland v Airedale AHA* (1993) that a person who is in a persistent vegetative state has no interests in being kept alive. Their lordships were clear that it was not contrary to the person's interests to be kept alive but it was not benefiting them either. This suggests that merely being kept alive is unlikely to be regarded as benefiting Mary. On the other hand, merely being kept alive is not regarded as benefiting her either. It may be crucial at that point to look at s 4, which requires treatment to be in the best interests of the patient. That might suggest that a neutral act is not permitted. Purely with that in mind, withdrawal of treatment may not be permitted but nor would putting her on the ventilator. But before we can reach that conclusion we must consider some other issues.

Second, the courts have made it clear that best interests should be considered broadly (*Re Wyatt (A Child) (Medical Treatment: Continuation of Order)* (2005)). It includes not only physical best interests but also social, emotional and family best interests.[12] This approach is confirmed in the Code of Practice for the **Mental Capacity Act 2005.**

Third, in considering what the best interests of a patient are, s 4 of the **Mental Capacity Act 2005** states that the court will consider their past wishes and feelings and their beliefs and values. This might be relevant in this case if it is determined that Mary wanted to have the baby, and had been willing to go through the process of pregnancy, with all its demands to date, although from this it would be wrong to assume that Mary would want to be kept artificially alive in order to keep the baby alive. Indeed her desire to produce the child may have been so that she could continue a relationship with the child, but that is no longer possible. The court may consider Mary's views about the fetus and what feelings she had towards it. Of course, this is a tricky issue to deal with because the precise turn of events is unlikely to have entered Mary's head and it would certainly be dangerous to assume that just because she had continued the pregnancy up until the accident she would want the ventilator kept on at this stage. Nevertheless, it is argued

---

11   Here the essay has set out the general test that will be applied (best interests) and then gone on to look at the particular factors that will be taken into account in applying it to the facts.

12   It is important to appreciate that 'best interests' is understood in a broad way.

that the fact she had maintained the pregnancy this far and was willing to make sacrifices for the fetus is evidence that is relevant for the best interest test.[13]

Fourth, there is the status of the fetus. For some people this will be the key issue. We need therefore to determine what the status of the fetus is in the eyes of the law. In short, the picture is unclear. It seems that the fetus is recognised as having some rights, but not as many as a person. It is a *sui generis*, protected in some way by the law, but short of being recognised as a person. We can see this by virtue of the fact that it is protected by the criminal law, for example by the offence of procuring a miscarriage, even though it is not treated as a person for the purposes of the criminal law (*Attorney-General's Reference (No 3 of 1994)* (1998)). Similarly, protection under civil law (e.g. **Congenital Disabilities (Civil Liability) Act 1976**) is possible for injuries done to the fetus, but only when the fetus is born as a person. However, it is submitted that these debates are in fact moot as regards Mary's situation. Under the **Mental Capacity Act 2005** it is not possible to do an act to Mary in order to benefit another, unless the act can be said to benefit Mary. So, even if we recognise the fetus as having some interests, they do not really affect the issue. Mary's treatment under the **Mental Capacity Act 2005** must be designed to promote Mary's best interests.[14]

Fifth, s 4 does allow us to consider the views of Mary's carers and family. Susan in this case thinks that Mary's best interests lie in her not being kept alive, but Tom disagrees. **Section 4** is clear that the views of the relatives or carers lie only in so far as they are evidence of what is in her best interests. So the court will not place weight on Tom or Susan's views in their own right but only in so far as they reveal what Mary's interests are. It should be emphasised that English law does not recognise 'proxy' decision-making, unless Mary has appointed a deputy. This is not mentioned in the facts and so it is assumed she has not.

Sixth, an argument might be made that the decision should be regarded as analogous to an abortion, so that the ventilator should only be switched off, thereby killing the fetus, if an abortion in such circumstances would be lawful. If that approach was taken the most plausible ground would be in **Abortion Act 1967, s 1(1)(a)** (available because the pregnancy has not exceeded its twenty-fourth week). It would need to be argued that there was a risk to the mental or physical health of Mary. However, given her state it would be hard to see how that could be shown. There might be an argument that her physical health will be affected by the physical manifestations of pregnancy, but if that were so then any pregnant woman would automatically fall within s 1(1)(a). It may be replied that an analogy with the **Abortion Act 1967** is not appropriate here, that it is not a question of

---

13 This paragraph is a good example of trying to show precisely how the law would be applied to the case at hand.

14 Remember that a woman's right to bodily integrity is not lost just because she is pregnant.

killing the fetus through the abortion, but whether medical treatment should or should not be given to Mary. Therefore the **Mental Capacity Act 2005** is the correct focus and that brings us back to the best interests of Mary.[15]

To conclude, the issue is likely to come down to an assessment of Mary's best interests as required under the **Mental Capacity Act 2005**. As shown above, that will require a number of features. Ultimately the court will need to decide whether her past wishes and beliefs indicate that she regarded producing a child as a good in itself or whether she would regard it to be undignified to be kept alive as a 'fetal container'.

QUESTION 18

Assess the law governing the sterilisation of those who lack capacity.

COMMENTARY

This is one of those issues which come up every now and again. It is not a 'cert' for a medical law paper. In revision you will need to decide whether to take a risk and revise carefully and you will be delighted if it comes up, or whether to give it a miss. There are not a huge number of cases and it may well be worthwhile being prepared to answer on this topic.

As usual you will need to show an awareness not only of the law, but also of the theoretical issues. An important point to emphasise is that nearly all of the case law was decided before the **Mental Capacity Act 2005** came into force. So you will need to address the question of whether the Act has changed the approach the law has taken.

How to Answer this Question

- ❖   Outline the key principles; note the **Mental Capacity Act**
- ❖   Factors indicating sterilisation appropriate
- ❖   Factors indicating sterilisation inappropriate
- ❖   The significance of the **Mental Capacity Act 2005**.

---

15   In a way the essay went off on a sidetrack, but it was necessary to explain why the interests of the fetus would not affect the key focus on the approach of the courts on the best interests of Mary.

Applying the Law

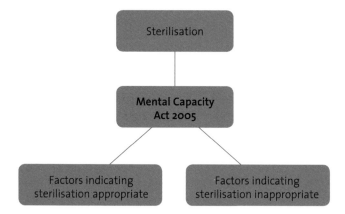

*The diagram illustrates the relationship between sterilisation and the **Mental Capacity Act** in this scenario.*

SUGGESTED ANSWER -

There has been a series of cases where the court has had to determine whether or not a person lacking capacity should be sterilised. This essay will consider this issue. While there are quite a few cases considering the issue, these have been heard prior to the passing of the **Mental Capacity Act 2005**. Later in this essay we will consider whether the **Mental Capacity Act** might be seen to have changed the law's approach to these cases.

It is difficult to avoid the issue of eugenics when discussing sterilisation. In the early part of the twentieth century in particular, sterilisation of those lacking mental capacity was seen as appropriate to avoid 'undesirables' producing even more undesirable children. Of course few were more enthusiastic about eugenic sterilisation than the Nazi regime. They sterilised up to 3.5 million people. It is understandable given its awful history that there is great sensitivity to the issue even today.[16]

The essay title asks us to discuss those who lack capacity, so our discussion will be limited to them. That will nowadays be governed by the **Mental Capacity Act 2005. Section 1** explains that decisions concerning those who lack capacity must be made in their best interests. This is not an area of the law where the *Bolam* test has application. It is not a question of whether a responsible body of medical opinion would support the procedure, but what is in the best interests of the individuals (*Re F (A Mental Patient: Sterilisation)* (1990)). The Code of Practice attached to the Act, produced by the Department of

- -

16 Here we are showing a good understanding of the historical background, which will please the examiner.

Constitutional Affairs, requires that an application be brought to court, at least in cases of non-therapeutic sterilisation.[17]

As already mentioned, the key test will be what is in the best interests of the individual patient. This indicates that eugenic considerations should not be taken into account. Even if it was considered that a certain group of people should not be permitted to reproduce for the good of society (a horrible thought), that would not justify their sterilisation. The focus must be on the individual themselves. The courts, in determining whether sterilisation is in a patient's best interests, are likely to refer to some of the case law that existed before the Act.

A leading decision is *Re B (A Minor) (Wardship: Sterilisation)* (1987) before the House of Lords. The decision concerned a girl who was aged 17, but with a mental age of a child aged 5 or 6. Their lordships highlighted the following factors in supporting her sterilisation:

- ❖ She would not understand pregnancy and would find it terrifying and distressing.
- ❖ She had no 'maternal instincts' and could not care for the child.
- ❖ The pain and difficulties of menstruation would be avoided.[18]

Interestingly in that case their lordships rejected the approach taken by the Canadian Supreme Court in *Re Eve* (1986). There the court had emphasised the importance of maintaining a person's physical integrity. A non-therapeutic sterilisation was a 'grave intrusion' on her rights and could not be justified. Lord Bridge thought such an approach was inconsistent with English law, which focused on best interests and not on more abstract rights to physical integrity. The **Mental Capacity Act 2005** would appear to reinforce Lord Bridge's approach.[19]

The courts have made it clear that they will not consider the interests of those caring for the person lacking capacity (*Re B* (1987)). The fact that sterilisation would make life easier for carers was not relevant. The fact that, were she to become pregnant, this would create additional burdens was not to be taken into account. It may be, however, that the court would listen to an argument if the carers could show that the difficulties of caring for the patient without sterilisation were so great that they would not be able to carry on caring without the sterilisation, and that without those carers the patient would suffer.

---

17 The Code of Practice is often, for those professionals working in the area, of more practical help than the statute.
18 This is a helpful and concise summary of the key points made in this case.
19 It is helpful to explain how the **Mental Capacity Act 2005** is likely to follow the approach taken by the earlier case law.

When looking at a patient's best interests the court will take into account the ethical, social, moral and broad welfare considerations. In *Re A (Medical Treatment: Male Sterilisation)* (2000) it was suggested that a court produce a checklist of the advantages and disadvantages of the sterilisation for the patient. These should be weighed up to determine what is in the best interests of the patient.

In considering these facts it is likely that weight will be attached to the views of the professionals involved. It is highly unlikely that a sterilisation would be approved without professional support. Indeed it is notable that in the few cases where permission for sterilisation was not granted, the professional opinion was divided (e.g. *Re LC* (1997)).

It seems that the courts start from a presumption against ordering sterilisation. It will need to be shown that sterilisation is a 'last resort' (*Re B* (1987)). In other words, it needs to be demonstrated that there is no less intrusive way of achieving the benefits of sterilisation, save sterilisation itself. In *Re A (Medical Treatment: Male Sterilisation)* (2000) it was said that sterilising a person without their consent could infringe their human rights under Arts 3 or 8 of the European Convention on Human Rights. Any infringement requires good justification and needs to be limited to the minimum necessary. For example, if it decides that pregnancy should be avoided, a court will need evidence that forms of contraception are not appropriate. In *Re P* (1989) this was justified because the woman concerned could not be trusted to take the pill regularly. In *Re Z (Medical Treatment: Hysterectomy)* (2000) it was said that sterilisation was necessary to deal with very painful periods. Critics suggest that these two cases indicate that it does not take much to persuade the court that sterilisation is necessary.

A common ground for wanting sterilisation is fear that the patient will become pregnant and be unable to deal with the pregnancy or look after the child. If this is the ground it must be shown that the risk of pregnancy is not fanciful. In *Re LC* (1997) Thorpe LJ found that LC's carers looked after her very well and so it was very unlikely she would become pregnant.

The courts, then, focus on the best interests of the patient. Where there are medical (therapeutic) grounds for sterilisation permission will readily be granted. Where the grounds are to avoid the problems with menstruation or pregnancy the court will require evidence that these are sufficient to justify the sterilisation and that there is no less interventionist way of protecting the individual.

There have certainly been complaints about the courts' approach. Jackson has criticised the courts for being far too ready to accept evidence that sterilisation should be used.[20] Although she approves of the language of last resort used by the courts, she is not

20 E. Jackson, *Regulating Reproduction*, Oxford: Hart, 2001.

convinced that it is reflected in practice. Certainly the best interests language is so vague that it enables the courts to consider a broad range of factors which justify a sterilisation.

Margot Brazier and Emma Cave express a powerful concern that sterilisation is used to cover up sexual abuse in institutional settings.[21] They believe that greater efforts should be made to ensure that those who lack capacity are not the victims of sexual assault. Sterilisation may be said to make the job of institutions easier because it will be less obvious if they are preventing individuals who lack capacity from having sex.[22]

Another concern is that the law is not gender neutral in its application. Although many women lacking capacity have been sterilised, in one of the few cases involving a man this was not approved (*Re A (Medical Treatment: Male Sterilisation)* (2000)). Although there was said to be risk of him impregnating women it was said not to be in his interests to be sterilised. This may reflect a rather narrow view of what best interests means.

To conclude, the current law is based on a straightforward assessment of best interests. We have not had any cases specifically on sterilisation since the **2005 Mental Capacity Act**. It may be that the focus in that legislation on best interests and restrictions on the use of force will mean that the courts will be less willing to authorise sterilisations than they were in the past. This may be particularly so following the **Human Rights Act**. However, a proper respect of the dignity and right to bodily integrity may involve not only leaving sterilisation as a last resort, but also ensuring that women who lack capacity are effectively protected from sexual assault.

Aim Higher ★

Consider whether the current law takes enough consideration of the concerns of the family and carers of the person lacking capacity. Given the day-to-day difficulties that they must endure, if they would find sterilisation would greatly ease their burden, should the law not assist them?

---

21 M. Brazier and E. Cave, *Medicine, Patients and the Law*, London: Penguin, 2011.

22 Making reference to some of the leading commentators will impress the examiner.

Assisted Reproduction

6

Checklist ✔

You need to be aware of

- The regulation of assisted reproduction
- How the law decides who is the mother in cases of assisted reproduction
- How the law decides who is the father in cases of assisted reproduction
- The law governing surrogacy
- When the law permits parents to select characteristics of their children

QUESTION 19

How does and should the law regulate surrogacy?

COMMENTARY

To answer this question it will be necessary to explain how the law currently regulates surrogacy and then sets out the debates over how the law should interact with surrogacy. Remember to do both or you will not score well.

It is a good idea to start by defining what surrogacy is. You will then want to set out the current law on surrogacy. Notice the word 'regulate' is used and so you will be discussing not only whether surrogacy should be lawful but also some of the other legal issues: should it be paid; who should be the child's parents; should it be subject to licensing?

When discussing the theory remember to separate the different issues.

How to Answer this Question

- ❖ Definition of surrogacy
- ❖ Current law on legality of surrogacy; commercialisation; parenthood
- ❖ Debates on legality of surrogacy
- ❖ Should commercial surrogacy be allowed?
- ❖ How should disputes over parenthood be resolved?

Applying the Law

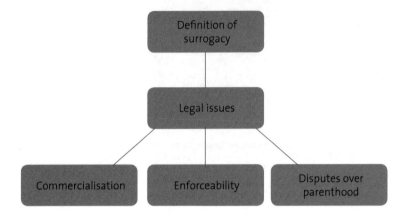

The diagram shows a range of key legal issues to consider for surrogacy in this context.

SUGGESTED ANSWER

Examples of surrogacy can be found in biblical times. It is hardly a recent phenomenon. It is generally understood to mean an arrangement whereby one woman will carry a child for another, on the understanding that the child will be handed over shortly after birth. In some cases the gametes of the commissioning person or couple are used to produce the child (sometimes known as partial surrogacy); in other cases the commissioning person or couple have no genetic link with the child (sometimes known as full surrogacy). Surrogacy is certainly not common in Britain, with up to 100 cases per year.

First, the current law on surrogacy will be set out, before examining some of the debates over the issue. It is not an offence to enter a surrogacy agreement itself, but it is unlawful to negotiate or arrange a surrogacy on a commercial basis. So a charity can make arrangements for surrogacy, but a company seeking to make profits cannot. It is unlawful for anyone to advertise surrogacy services, but it is permissible to ask in your Christmas cards whether your friends would be willing to be surrogates. It is unlawful to offer a reward or profit to the gestational mother, although she can be offered money for her expenses. These provisions are all found in the **Surrogacy Arrangements Act 1985**.

A surrogacy contract is not enforceable. That is clear from **Surrogacy Arrangements Act 1985, s 1A**. If a woman gives birth to a child following a surrogacy arrangement she is the mother of the child. That follows the normal rules on the allocation of motherhood (**s 33 Human Fertilisation and Embryology Act 2008 (HFE Act 2008)**). If the mother refuses to hand over the child the commissioning parents can apply for a residence order, but unless the mother poses a risk to the child it would be very unlikely that they would succeed (*Re Q (A Minor) (Parental Order)* (1996)). That is because the law tends to assume that the 'natural mother' is the best person to bring up a child. If, however, the mother is happy to hand the child over to the commissioning couple then they can become the parents of the child in one of two ways. They could apply for a parental order under s 54 of the HFE Act 2008. This will be granted if a number of factors are shown, including that the mother consents, that the making of the order is in the best interests of the child and one of the commissioning parents has a genetic link to the child. Alternatively they could apply to adopt the child.

There are two main issues relating to surrogacy. The first is whether the law should encourage or permit it. The second is how the law should deal with a dispute over the child following birth.

Looking first at whether the law should encourage or permit surrogacy. As we have seen, the law takes a somewhat lukewarm attitude to surrogacy. It is not unlawful, but surrogacy cannot be advertised or paid for; and a surrogacy arrangement cannot be enforced. The arguments in favour of surrogacy are as follows. First, it is based on autonomy. If the woman wishes to be a surrogate mother and a couple wish to employ her, why should they not be able to? They are not harming anyone else. Indeed the production of a baby will be a joy to many. Second, it is said that we should simply accept that surrogacy will happen. It has occurred since biblical times and so it is unlikely that the law could prohibit it. Any attempt to render surrogacy unlawful is likely to simply send it underground. Third, it is said that surrogacy has a liberalising effect on society. It enables same-sex couples or single men to arrange for a child to be cared for. People who otherwise could not readily have a child who would be theirs can have one through surrogacy.

Those who oppose surrogacy tend to make the following points. First, that surrogacy is harmful to the child. A child produced through surrogacy may feel they have been created in circumstances in which they were treated as a commodity to be bought and sold. Further, surrogacy arrangements are said to be a recipe for disputes and litigation. A surrogate mother may well, upon the birth, decide not to hand the child over and then litigation will follow which is bound to be unsettling for the child. Alternatively, the commissioning couple may refuse to accept the child and that is likely to lead to the child having to go into care. It is better not to allow this volatile way of producing children. Against this it may be pointed out that the studies suggest that disputes following a surrogacy are rare (see the statistics in the Brazier Report[1]).

A second argument against surrogacy is that it exploits surrogates. There is some evidence of this in the United States, where surrogates are paid and there are suggestions that some women undertake surrogacy work to pay off debts. However, under the English non-commercial system it is hard to see why it is exploitation to be a surrogate.

1   M. Brazier, *Surrogacy: Review for Health Ministers*, London: Department of Health, 1998.

A third argument is that the practice of surrogacy becomes close to baby-selling or baby-donating. The concern seems to be that it involves treating a child a little like a commodity to be transferred. Again this is a stronger concern in cases of commercial surrogacy. It perhaps overlooks the great expense that parents undertake to have children in more traditional ways.

So it is submitted that there are few strong concerns with surrogacy where it is non-commercial and that the current approach of allowing non-commercial surrogacy is appropriate. There are greater concerns with commercial surrogacy that women will be pressurised into it, but that might be said to be true of a wide range of unpleasant jobs that people do.

Turning to the issue of enforceability, it is submitted that the current approach of the law is correct. Through the pregnancy and labour the gestational mother will have undertaken a huge amount of work and bodily invasion in order to produce the child. She has cared for the child during the pregnancy and arguably formed a bond with the child during that time. Her work and effort give her a far stronger claim to the child than the commissioning parent, whose effort will have been little by comparison. Where the surrogate hands the child over the situation is less straightforward. It is commonly assumed that if the surrogate does not want the child the commissioning couple should have her, but there is an argument for saying that the local authority should consider whether the commissioning couple are as good as the couple at the front of the queue for adopting the child. If the commissioning couple do not have a genetic link with the child a child-centred approach would ask who will be the best parent for this child, and while that may be the commissioning couple, there may be others who will be better equipped to look after the child. Certainly if the commissioning couple have a genetic link or are the best alternative parents then the law is right to provide, through a parental order or adoption, an effective way of them becoming the parents of the child in the eyes of the law.

> ### Aim Higher ★
> An issue to explore is whether surrogacy is more degrading or more likely to lead to exploitation than other activities which people who are desperate for money engage in. Goold has argued that, in fact, poor people may be even worse off if they are denied the opportunity to use surrogacy and so outlawing surrogacy weakens rather than strengthens their position.[2]

---

2   I. Goold, 'Surrogacy: Is There a Case for Legal Prohibition?', 12(2) *Journal of Law and Medicine*, 2004, 205–16.

QUESTION 20

How does the law determine who is the parent of a child in a case of assisted reproduction and how should it do so?

COMMENTARY

This question falls neatly into two halves. First, describing how the law allocates parenthood in cases of assisted reproduction; and second, discussing how the law should operate in this area.

Remember that the law has been significantly changed by the **Human Fertilisation and Embryology Act 2008 (HFE Act 2008)**. Make sure you are up to date and use the correct provisions. Confusingly, there are still some provisions of the **Human Fertilisation and Embryology Act 1990** which remain relevant.

How to Answer this Question

- ❖ General principles of the law on parenthood
- ❖ Defining motherhood in cases of assisted reproduction
- ❖ Defining fatherhood in cases of assisted reproduction
- ❖ Discussion of the principles of allocation of parentage: biology v social.

Answer Structure

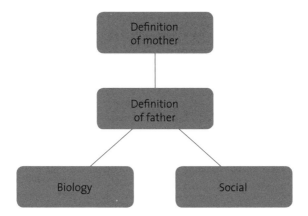

SUGGESTED ANSWER

The normal principles by which it is decided who is the mother or father of a child are relatively straightforward in English law. The mother of a child is the woman who gives birth to him or her. The father is the genetic father. However, once assisted reproductive technologies enter the picture the situation all becomes rather murky! In this essay we will set out the basic principles of the current law and then move on to a discussion of what they ought to be.

Section 33 of the **HFE Act 2008** states that the woman who gives birth to the child is the mother, even if she became pregnant using donated eggs. She may, therefore, not have a genetic tie to the child, but it is through the pregnancy and the giving birth that she becomes entitled to be known as the mother of the child. To be clear, the woman who donated the eggs would not be the mother.

If donated sperm is used outside the context of a licensed clinic the normal rules apply. That means that a genetic father is the legal father. So a man should not become involved in a 'DIY' insemination unless he is happy to be the father. The following rules only apply where the procedures take place within a licensed clinic.

A man who donates his sperm to a clinic under the terms set out in **Sch 3** of the **HFE Act 2008** is not to be treated as the father of a child. That is made clear by **s 41 HFE Act 2008**. That means that a sperm donor to a licensed clinic need have no fears that he will subsequently be liable to pay child support.

Section 35 of the **HFE Act 2008** states that if a married woman gives birth using donated sperm then her husband will be the father of any child born unless he can show two things: that he is not the genetic father and that he did not consent to the placing of the embryo in her. All clinics will require the written consent of a married patient's husband to receiving treatment so it should be very rare for this exception to apply. It means that if a couple go for licensed treatment and a child is produced they will be the parents of the child, even if neither of them is genetically related to the child.

Section 42 states that the provisions just discussed in relation to husbands operate in the same way for civil partners. So if two women civil partners receive treatment the one who gives birth will be the mother and the other will be a parent of the child. Notably, the partner will not be technically the mother of the child, but rather the parent. No legal significance turns on this, but it seems Parliament felt uncomfortable about the idea that a child might have two mothers.

If the mother is not married and does not have a civil partner but lives with someone, then they too can be a parent of the child. That is so if the 'agreed parenthood conditions' apply. These are found in **s 44 HFE Act 2008**. They apply equally to a male or female partner. To satisfy the 'agreed parenthood conditions' it must be shown that the woman and the partner have given written signed notice to the clinic agreeing that the partner will be the parent; that the consents have not been withdrawn; that the woman has not given consent for any other person to be the legal parent; and that the woman and her partner are not within the prohibited degrees of relationship. If the woman is with a male partner he will be the father; if with a female partner she will be a parent, but again not officially the mother.

It is interesting to note that these rules mean that a child cannot have more than one mother or father. This insistence is a little odd as two men or women can adopt a child and thereby both become mothers or fathers. Notably it is also possible for a child to have no father. That would arise where a single woman becomes pregnant at a licensed clinic using donated sperm.

One final point that is worth making is that if the rules as described do not apply then the fallback position is that the genetic father is the father. In *Leeds Teaching Hospital v A* (2003) a mix-up occurred at a clinic and Mrs A's eggs were mixed with Mr B's sperm, instead of her husband's. The court concluded that Mr B was the father of the child as the provisions relating to sperm donors did not relate to him. He was the genetic father and the fact he had no intention of being a father of a child with Mrs A was no defence.

Having set out these rules we can consider whether they are appropriate. This takes us back to the fundamental question of what makes someone the parent of a child. For some it is the genetic link which is crucial. They (e.g. Bainham[3]) point out that other people who might have a legitimate say in the child's upbringing can be awarded parental responsibility (which will give the holder the rights and responsibilities of parenthood), but insist that parentage itself should be restricted to the actual biological link. For them the principles in the **HFE Act** are misguided. It is important for children to know who their biological parents are. The **HFE Act** provisions create a fiction about the origins of the child. Such concerns are bolstered by the fact that many parents who have children by using assisted reproduction do not inform their children of their biological origins. Supporters of the genetic link would explain that we could say that a sperm donor is the father of the child, but put in place special provision which would mean he could not exercise the rights of a father, and granting the woman's husband parental responsibility to recognise the role he will play in the child's life.

Others argue that what makes someone a parent is not the biological link but the day-to-day care of the child. It is the doing of the work of parenthood which means a person knows the child well and will have the best interests of the child at heart. The brief interlude of donating sperm is not enough to make someone a parent; the changing of nappies and comforting of the crying baby will do so. They would be generally supportive of the provisions in the **HFE Act** because those ensure that the person who is likely to be most involved in the child's life is recognised as the parent of the child. We can assume that the sperm donor will not see the child so he does not get parenthood, but we can predict that the husband will be involved in the child's life and so he is given parenthood.

---

3   A. Bainham, 'Arguments about parentage', 67 *Cambridge Law Journal*, 2008, 322.

A third view is that we should focus on causation. Rebecca Probert has argued that the HFE Act shows that those most involved in a causal sense are regarded as the parents.[4] It is true that the sperm donor has contributed to the creation of a child, but his mere deposit of sperm only leads to a child because the woman or couple then use it to create a child together. Others are not convinced by this argument. They argue that it is not clear why the partner or husband of the woman plays more of a causal role than the sperm donor.

As can be seen, one's views on the allocation of parenthood depend much on what one regards as central to the notion of what makes a person a parent. It is submitted that the HFE Act seems largely to reflect the notion of social parent. It is based on who we can predict will play the social role of parent in the child's life. We can recognise the biological link in other ways, through registers of sperm donation and the like. As for who should be the actual parent, the law seems to ask who will the child call Mum and Dad. That is a pretty good place to start.

> **Common Pitfalls**
> Although the **2008 Act** has removed the need to consider the need for a father, remember that the clinic must still consider the welfare of the child in deciding whether to offer treatment services.

QUESTION 21

How does and should the law restrict access to assisted reproduction?

COMMENTARY

You need to think carefully about the question that is asked here. Notice that the focus is on how the law restricts access. You will want to consider what restrictions there are on access to assisted reproduction. But don't be misled into thinking you are not meant to consider practical restrictions. If the law were to grant a right to assisted reproduction then the accessibility of assisted reproduction would be very different. Indeed it might be a useful approach to ask yourself how it would be different if we had an unfettered right to assisted reproduction.

It is important to be aware of the changes to the **1990 Human Fertilisation and Embryology Act** by the **2008 Act** of the same title. Notice too the impact of the **Human Rights Act** on these issues.

---

4   R. Probert, 'Families, assisted reproduction and the law', 16 *Child and Family Law Quarterly*, 2004, 273.

How to Answer this Question

❖ Concepts of reproductive autonomy and human rights arguments
❖ Statutory restrictions
❖ Same-sex couples
❖ Age restrictions
❖ Rationing and financial restrictions.

Answer Structure

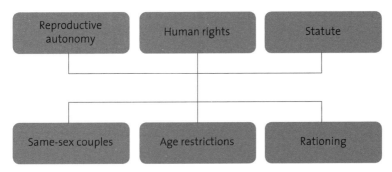

When devising an answer here it is important to consider the relationships between these legal and social factors.

SUGGESTED ANSWER

In recent years there has been no suggestion that assisted reproduction should be unlawful. Quite the opposite: it has become a well-recognised part of the National Health Service. However, it is clear that there are plenty of people who wish to access the services who cannot. In this essay we shall examine what restrictions apply in accessing assisted reproduction.

Before looking at these it is helpful to consider the theoretical issues. The debate over access to assisted reproductive services tends to focus on the notion of reproductive autonomy. It is worth distinguishing two ways in which that term could be understood: reproductive liberty and reproductive autonomy. The notion of reproductive liberty is that one's reproductive choices (when, where, how and with whom a person has children) are an intimate matter in which the state should not interfere. The State should not seek to restrict someone's reproduction on the basis that they are an unsuitable person. However, this is a negative concept: it is telling the State to keep out of reproductive choices. The concept of reproductive autonomy is often seen as more positive. Decisions about whether or not to have children are profoundly important and intimate for individuals and are central as to how they wish to live their lives. There is an obligation on the State to do what it can to assist individuals to pursue intimate projects. This is particularly so where disability or illness would otherwise prevent them from achieving these goals.

We shall start by looking at the legal restrictions on who can access assisted reproductive services. **Section 13(5)** of the **Human Fertilisation and Embryology Act 1990** (HFE Act 1990) states that:

> A woman shall not be provided with treatment services unless account has been taken of the welfare of any child who may be born as a result of the treatment (including the need of that child for supportive parenting, and of any other child who may be affected by the birth).

This requires the clinic to consider the welfare of any child that will be born before offering treatment. In particular, consideration is to be given to the need of the child for supportive parenting and the needs of any other child for supportive parenting. This provision has proved controversial. It was amended by the **HFE Act 2008**, which deleted the requirement for clinics to consider the need of a child for a father. That provision was seen as creating a barrier to assisted reproductive services for single women or lesbian couples (Riley).[5] The amended wording might still operate to bar a single woman who did not have a network of friends or family who could assist in the care of the child.

It is difficult to know what clinics make of the **s 13(5)** test. As Emily Jackson has pointed out, trying to imagine the welfare of a child who does not yet exist is a mind-boggling test.[6] Indeed it might be argued that it would very rarely be in the child's interests not to be born. Notably the **HFE Act** Code suggests that the clinic consider whether the child to be born will be at risk of suffering significant harm or neglect. That suggests that it would be very rare that a clinic would use **s 13(5)** to deny access to treatment. The House of Commons Science and Technology Committee found that in less than 0.3 per cent of cases was this provision used, and that was under the old wording of the Act.

The bar is controversial. Earlier we introduced the concepts of reproductive liberty and autonomy and they are relevant here. Both concepts are not absolute claims and accept that the state can intervene or fail to provide services where there is harm to others. There is nothing at all unusual about restricting autonomy or liberty where that is necessary to avoid harm to others. It might be argued that in **s 13(5)** that is what is being done: the reproductive autonomy of the couple is restricted in order to protect the child from harm. This seems convincing, save for the argument that it is impossible to predict whether a child will suffer harm or not and that we should not interfere with autonomy based on speculation. It may, at this point of the debate, be relevant whether we are talking about the provision of State services or private services. It may be argued that a vague risk of harm is insufficient to interfere in reproductive liberty (if a couple are paying

5   L. Riley, 'Equality of access to NHS-funded IVF treatment in England and Wales', in K. Horsey and H. Biggs (eds) *Human Fertilization and Embryology: Reproducing Regulation*, London: Routledge, 2007.

6   E. Jackson, *Regulating Reproduction*, Oxford: Hart, 2001.

for their own treatment), but is sufficient to interfere in reproductive autonomy (if a couple are seeking a positive claim for treatment).

The argument against s 13(5) can be strengthened by a reference to a claim that there is discrimination. Amel Alghrani and John Harris have argued that fertile couples have complete freedom to reproduce whenever they wish.[7] There is no need for them to be approved by a clinic and no one determines the welfare of any child they will produce. They argue that the fact that we restrict access for infertile couples is a form of discrimination. In other areas of disability law the state seems to put in place accommodations so that people are not treated differently as a result of their disability. There are a number of responses to this argument. Some reject the claim that being unable to have children without assistance is a disability. A disability involves being prevented from performing functions which are central to life. Fertility, it is said, is a luxury. You may not be able to play the violin well, but that is not a disability. These arguments all turn on whether you see an inability to reproduce without medical assistance as interfering with a key part of life. An alternative response to Alghrani and Harris's argument is to say that the State should, in the name of child protection, prevent children being produced by couples in circumstances where the child will suffer serious harm. We cannot do this in cases where parents are fertile, but where we can (i.e. where they lack fertility) we should. Alghrani and Harris take their argument to its logical conclusion and argue that even if two known child abusers seek assistance from a clinic we should offer them services. As they point out, if they were fertile we would not stop them having children. That may be going too far for some! There is a third argument here and this is that in cases of assisted reproduction the clinic is playing a role in the creation of a child and therefore has a responsibility toward the child. The clinic should rightly consider the child's future therefore and decline to actively participate in a procedure which will lead to serious harm to the child. It is submitted that a clinic should take responsibility for the result of its actions: the creation of a child. **Section 13(5)** is correct in requiring the clinic to ensure that the child will not be at risk of suffering significant harm. There are three particular issues we shall now consider.

The first is lesbian couples. When the **HFE Act 1990** was first passed there were significant debates over whether lesbian couples should be allowed to receive assisted reproductive treatment. However, it is now widely accepted that a lesbian couple can offer just as good parenting as an opposite-sex couple. Indeed, one study by Brewaeys found a greater involvement of both parents in the child's life in lesbian couples than in opposite-sex couples.[8] This is recognised in the **Adoption and Children Act 2002**, which

7   A. Alghrani and J. Harris, 'Reproductive liberty: should the foundation of families be regulated?', 18 *Child and Family Law Quarterly*, 2006, 191.

8   A. Brewaeys, 'Lesbian couples in DI practice', in J. Gunning and H. Szoke (eds) *The Regulation of Assisted Reproductive Technology*, Aldershot: Ashgate, 2003.

permits same-sex couples to adopt children. So it seems now there is no reason to deny lesbian couples access to assisted reproduction, based on their sexuality.

More debate surrounds single women seeking assisted reproductive treatment. Many of the arguments made above can be repeated. For example, it is said that a fertile single woman can seek a one-night stand and become pregnant, so if a woman wants (or prefers) assisted reproduction why should she be treated differently? As argued above, there is a case for acknowledging the responsibility the clinic has as a result of its active role in creating the child. The clinic will want to ensure that any couple or single person has the resources they need to be able to care for a child. No doubt a single person can, especially if supported by family and friends, raise a child.

Moving next on to the availability of assisted reproductive resources. Although the NHS does provide assisted reproductive services, only around 25 per cent of IVF treatment is funded by the NHS; most of it is provided by the private sector. In the private sector it is expensive, costing around £8,000 per cycle. The extent to which the state should provide assisted reproductive services depends on whether one believes the case is made for reproductive autonomy as well as reproductive liberty, as set out above.

The National Institute for Health and Clinical Excellence (NICE) has recently reviewed the provision of services and has recommended that a woman be offered up to three cycles of IVF if she is between 23 and 39 years old and she has an identified cause for fertility problems or infertility of at least three years' duration. Despite the issuing of these guidelines a study by Schapps found that in eight out of ten areas in the country this guidance was not followed and lower provision of IVF was offered.[9] Notably, the Department of Health has accepted that not all PCTs can meet the NICE guidelines in full. They recommend that for women between 23 and 39 a single cycle of IVF be offered, while the NHS tries to move towards meeting the NICE guidelines.

This is a controversial area and many have spoken out against the limited provision for assisted reproduction available on the NHS. It is notable how rates of IVF generally are much lower than in comparable EU countries. The sad truth is that in England many people are not able to become parents because they are unable to afford it. We should, however, not forget that in essence we are discussing a rationing issue here. If money were in place to fund extensive cycles of IVF that would mean there would be less money to meet other demands on the NHS. How are we to compare the need to provide hip replacements and to provide IVF?

....

9   G. Schapps, 'The IVF postcode lottery: Don't promise what you can't deliver', *Bionews*, 9 August 2009.

One issue raised by the NICE guidelines relates to age. Even under the NICE guidelines a woman aged over 39 would not be entitled to NHS treatment. In *R v Sheffield AHA ex p Seale* (1994) a woman aged 35 was denied assisted reproductive treatment on the basis of her age. This was justified on the basis that the chances of the treatment succeeding were greatly reduced once a woman reached the age of 35. As the law develops its response to age discrimination this issue is likely to be raised again. As long as the medical evidence supports the claim it is likely that discrimination against older women in the provision of NHS treatment will be justified. It will be seen as a sensible rationing decision to deny treatment which has a low likelihood of success. However, that will not be an argument against allowing a woman who is seeking private treatment. Recently a 67-year-old became pregnant in Romania. In the case of private treatment it should only be concerns about the welfare of the child which justify denying access to assisted reproductive treatment.

To conclude, this is undoubtedly a controversial and tricky area. At the heart of the debate is the role of the State in reproductive decisions. Is this an area where the State has a positive obligation to assist couples with fertility problems, or is the role of the State simply not to interfere? That in turn depends in part on whether infertility is regarded as equivalent to a disability: are children a luxury or a necessity?

QUESTION 22

Consider when parents can, and should, be able to select embryos pre-implantation.

COMMENTARY

The question of PGD ('pre-genetic diagnosis') has become a very hot topic. It enables parents to find out information about embryos before implantation and then choose which embryo to implant. The essay question asks you to discuss two things. The first is to discuss the extent to which the law regulates PGD and embryo selection. The second is to discuss the ethical disputes over this issue.

The law on this area was reformed by the **Human Fertilisation and Embryology Act 2008** and you will want to make sure that your answers are up to date.

How to Answer this Question
- ❖ Explain the practice of embryo selection
- ❖ The law as set out in the **HFE Act 2008**
- ❖ Disability arguments
  - ❖ Sex selection
  - ❖ Trivial factors
  - ❖ Saviour siblings.

Answer Structure

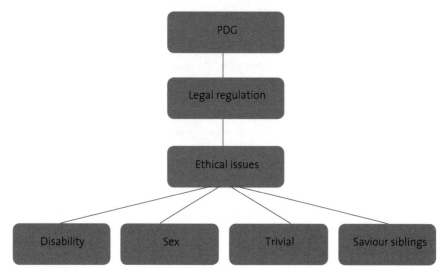

The relationship between regulation and the ethical issues explored in the answer is shown here.

SUGGESTED ANSWER ------------------------------

Couples using IVF typically create a number of embryos and then implant two at a time, in the hope of becoming pregnant. This essay asks us to consider when it is permissible to select between the embryos which will be implanted, or whether two should be selected at random. It is generally accepted that it is not controversial to suggest that if an embryo is not viable, it should not be selected. However, there is fierce debate over whether disability, sex or personal characteristics can be used to make the selection. That would involve PGD (pre-implantation genetic diagnosis) to find out more information about the embryos.

The **Human Fertilisation and Embryology Act 1990**, as amended by the **Human Fertilisation and Embryology Act 2008**, restricts the use of PGD. It can only be carried out with a licence from the Human Fertilisation and Embryology Authority (HFEA). The Act explain that PGD can be used only 'to establish if an embryo has an abnormality that might affect its capacity to result in a live birth' and 'to avoid a serious medical condition'. What amounts to a serious medical condition is detailed in a Code of Practice issued by the HFEA. This sets out a restrictive list of what kinds of medical conditions. The Code also explains that it is possible to use the sex of the embryo to make a selection where the embryo may suffer from a 'gender related serious disability, illness or medical condition'. This is a reference to a condition which will affect, say, girls more, or more often, than boys. So far the HFEA has licensed over 100 medical conditions, but has restricted this to the most serious ones.

Opinion on the correct approach to this issue is debated. There are some who think that the law should be far more willing to permit the use of PGD, while others believe that the current law is too generous. It is helpful to look at the different reasons people may have for wanting to use PGD.

First, let us consider the issue of disability. To some this is a straightforward issue. Why should a couple have to implant a disabled embryo, when they could implant one without a disability? What is the point in implanting a disabled embryo if the couple will be free to carry out an abortion later? Far better, the Human Genetics Commission have argued, to find out early on if there is a disability. Indeed you might even go further, as Julian Savulescu has gone, and argue that parents have a moral obligation to select the 'best' embryo. We would criticize parents who did not do the best for their children when born, we should do the same in the case of embryo selection.

Despite these arguments there is a case against selection, even for disability. If a couple choose from their embryos those which do not carry a gene for, say, cystic fibrosis, we can presume that those embryos carrying this gene will be discarded. But what does that say about the attitude revealed towards people suffering from cystic fibrosis? Is it not revealing a discriminatory attitude: in the most obvious way, the statement is that a life with cystic fibrosis is not worth as much as a fully healthy person's life? Does it not, as Adrianne Asche has argued, perpetuate the promotion of the myth of idealism as to human nature: that any child which is not perfect can be rejected by a parent?

While these are powerful arguments, it is suggested they should not lead to the conclusion that PGD should not be permitted. A parent who is selecting a non-disabled embryo over a disabled embryo is not saying that disabled people are 'better off dead', but rather that given a choice between having a disability and not having a disability, most people would rather not have the disability. Further, the parent is simply making an assessment that for their family, it will be better for the child not to have a disability; they may not be making a statement about disabled people generally.

The issue of sex selection is another controversial issue. As already mentioned, the HFEA does not allow embryo selection, unless there is a genetic illness, related to sex. Social factors, such as ensuring that the family has an equal number of boys and girls, is not permitted. Supporters are likely to rely on the autonomy argument, already mentioned, that parents should be free to select the children they want. Opponents of sex selection are concerned about the impact on society of allowing sex selection. We may end up with many more members of one sex than the other and that could have harmful social consequences. There may be harm for the children born, who will feel that they were only chosen because of their sex. Or there may be concerns that to allow sex selection will permit people to express their sexist beliefs. I agree, for these arguments, that the law should be very reluctant to allow the use of sex factors to select an embryo.

What about using trivial factors such as hair or eye colour? John Harris sees the selection of embryos as an individual choice for a woman, as part of her reproductive autonomy. If a woman, who is not infertile, can choose to have sex with a ginger haired man in the hope of having a ginger haired child, why should not an infertile woman be able to select the hair colour she wishes for her embryo. Rosamund Scott has argued that the interests of parents in choosing trivial characteristics is not strong and might encourage parents to take an inappropriate view of what being a parent is about. I agree. You should love the child you are given; not create the child you want to live.

One controversial issue is saviour siblings. This refers to a case where parents of a sick child wish to have another child whose tissue can be used to provide a treatment for the condition of their sick sibling. In *Quintavalle (on behalf of Comment on Reproductive Ethics) v HFEA* [2005] UKHL the House of Lords confirmed that the **HFEA** could licence PGD for the purposes of creating a saviour sibling. This has been confirmed in statute, through amendments to Para 1ZA of Sch 2 of the **Human Fertilisation and Embryology Act 1990**. These make it clear that only saviour siblings are allowed. Saviour cousins, would not be. The paragraph makes it clear that the Authority must consider the impact on the child who is to be born in deciding whether to permit the creation of a saviour sibling.

It is submitted that the law has struck the current balance correctly. Where the harm to the saviour sibling is limited and where the life of the other child will be saved or serious disability avoided, this is a reasonable part of family life.

Critics of 'saviour siblings' claim that it involves bringing a person into being for the sole purpose of assisting their sibling. This infringes the principle that people should not be used solely as a means to an end. There are two good replies to this. One is that in fact to save the life of one's sibling is beneficial to the donor, or at least not harmful to them. The second is that it is extremely unlikely that parents would treat the saviour sibling simply as a source of tissue. It would be hard to believe that parents would 'discard' a saviour sibling once treatment of the existing child had been effective.

To conclude, the law only permits PGD and the selection of embryos when there is a very good reason for doing so: to avoid a serious disability. There are grave dangers if PGD and embryo selection was allowed for trivial reasons. The current law is, therefore, taking the best approach.

Aim Higher ★

Some disabled couples have sought to select an embryo with a disability. Consider whether they should be allowed to do so. Is there an argument that for, say, a couple of restricted growth if they were to have a child of normal size that child would, in their family, be disabled?

Ownership of Bodies

7

Checklist ✔

You need to be aware of

- The current case law on the ownership of bodies
- The regulation provided by the **Human Tissue Act**
- When organs can be donated while a person is alive
- The debate over organ selling
- When organs can be used from a deceased person
- The ethical debates over organ donation

QUESTION 23

To what extent does the law recognise property interests in bodies or body parts?

COMMENTARY

This question is asking you about what the law is. You are not therefore expected to go into great detail about the theoretical issues surrounding body ownership. However, in the suggested answer you will see I do this a bit in order to explain the difficulties the law faces and why it has developed the way it has. The primary focus should be on the current law.

Make sure you are familiar with the recent *Yearworth* decision. This has really transformed the legal landscape on this issue.

How to Answer this Question

- ❖ Introduction to the main themes
- ❖ The law on body ownership
- ❖ The law on ownership of body parts pre-*Yearworth*
- ❖ The law on ownership of body parts post-*Yearworth*
- ❖ Why the law struggles with this issue.

Answer Structure

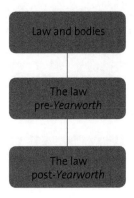

SUGGESTED ANSWER

There has been considerable debate in recent years over whether people own their bodies or parts of their bodies. This is, in part, because there is now much more commercial value in body parts and so the issue has become more prominent. Further, there seems to be greater concern over how doctors treat parts of removed bodies, which might reflect the decline in paternalistic approaches to medicine. There is usually a distinction drawn between ownership of your whole body and ownership of removed parts of the body.[1] So these will be dealt with separately.

The traditional rule was that there is no ownership in an intact body. Although that has commonly been said to represent the law (see e.g. *AB v Leeds Teaching Hospital NHS Trust* (2004)), as Roger Magnusson has argued, there is in fact very little direct authority on the issue.[2] In a way that is not surprising as it is only when a part of a body is removed that there is likely to be a dispute over ownership or use. It is in relation to corpses that the issue might arise, but there are public interest issues concerning the proper disposal of corpses, the proper recording of death, and ensuring that, where necessary, post mortems can be performed, that mean that the issue is rarely considered.[3]

What about separate parts of the body? Here there is more debate to be had. As we shall see, the issue has recently been reconsidered by the Court of Appeal in *Yearworth v North Bristol NHS Trust* (2009). But to understand that case it is necessary to look at the law

---

1   This is an important distinction for this topic. You will want to highlight that you have appreciated its significance.

2   R. Magnusson, 'Property rights in human corpses', in N. Palmer and E. McKendrick (eds) *Interests in Goods*, London: LL P, 1998.

3   Normally you would not want to spend time talking about the history of the law, but in this case it is necessary to have a brief summary so that you can explain the significance of *Yearworth*

prior to the courts' decision. The general rule seemed to be that body parts could not be owned, subject to a number of exceptions. These included in relation to the law on theft where a person has been convicted of the theft of hair (*R v Herbert* (1961)); blood (*R v Rothery* (1976)); or urine (*R v Welsh* (1975)). These cases could be dismissed as examples of the criminal law of theft departing from the normal civil law when necessary to render illegal conduct which was clearly blameworthy and contrary to the public interest. Perhaps of more significance is *R v Kelly* (1998) and *Dobson v North Tyneside Health Authority* (1996), in which it was held that if 'work and skill' had been exercised upon a part of a body then the person who used that work and skill could become the owner of it. So if, as in those cases, a part of a body was removed and the hospital exercised work and skill on the body part to preserve it then the body part could become property and owned by the hospital. Quite what amounted to work and skill was not clear. Indeed, in *AB v Leeds Teaching Hospital NHS Trust* (2004) Gage J accepted that the law was unclear and uncertain.

Since then we have the decision in *Yearworth*. Although, to be honest, it has done little to make the law clearer, it seems to have set a new course for the law. The case involved six men who had been diagnosed with cancer. They were due to receive chemotherapy and it was recommended that they provide samples of sperm because the treatment was likely to render them infertile. The sperm was frozen and stored by the hospital, but due to an error it was not kept at the correct temperature. The sperm therefore became useless. The men suffered psychological harm as a result.

The difficulty they faced was that there had not been an injury to their bodies and so a personal injury claim in tort was not available. That left a claim that their property had been damaged and a claim in bailment. The Court of Appeal accepted that the traditional analysis would have meant such a claim would fail because they could not claim ownership in their sperm. Indeed it would seem that using the work and skill exception, if anyone had ownership of the sperm it was the hospital, a conclusion which was of no help for the men's claim. However, the Court of Appeal held that there was a need for a 're-analysis' of the common law's treatment of the issue. It was clear the court thought that the men ought to have a remedy in this case and the fact that the law on body ownership appeared to be a stumbling block led to a re-examination of the law.

The Court of Appeal was critical of the work and skill exception. They did not believe it had a strong historical precedent and indeed they thought the distinction between parts of bodies which had been subject to skill and those which had not was 'not entirely logical'. Further, it does not always lead to the correct allocation of ownership. In this case surely it was the men, rather than the hospital, who should have had ownership of the sperm.

The Court of Appeal then set out five reasons why they thought the men had ownership of the sperm:

1. The men had created the sperm through their bodies and had caused it to be removed from their bodies.

2. The sole object of the ejaculation of the sperm was that the men could use it later on. This was not an accidental removal of a body part. It was deliberately done for a particular plan.

3. The storage was performed by the hospital for the benefit of the men. It was not storage for research or education. Further, the storage was performed under the **Human Fertilisation and Embryology Act 1990**.

4. The **1990 Act** put restrictions on how a licensing body could store gametes and this made it clear that the clinic was not to be treated as having ownership of the sperm.

5. There was a combination of the fact that the men had created the sperm; the sperm was stored for their use; and the clinic was under statutory duties in how it dealt with the sperm. These all pointed to ownership.

The Court of Appeal clearly thought that these points together generated a sufficient case to conclude that the men had a property interest in the sperm. In defrosting the sperm the clinic was breaching the terms of the bailment and so the men were entitled to recover damages. However, the case leaves the future direction of the law unclear.[4]

Let us start with what is certain. It seems now that people may in some circumstances be able to claim ownership in separated parts of their body. It also seems to be clear that the work and skill exception has been rejected. But moving beyond that the future is uncertain. In particular it is unclear whether all five of the criteria mentioned in *Yearworth* need to be satisfied before the body part can become property. A narrow reading would focus on the obligations imposed by the **Human Fertilisation and Embryology Act 1990** which played a significant role in the court's thinking. That would mean that the decision has a rather narrow precedent. An alternative reading would focus on the requirements that the body part be stored for an individual's particular purpose, which would give it a far wider significance. Time will tell how the law develops.[5]

It is clear that the law's interaction with the body is uncertain and it is worth briefly commenting on why this is so. First, there is the theoretical difficulty of how a person can own themselves. The nature of ownership is that the owner is different from the thing owned. This argument seems a more powerful objection to the ownership of an intact body than in relation to a removed body part. Second, there is the concern that if bodies are treated as property this will lead to the commercialisation of bodies. Bodies should be regarded as special, sacred even, and beyond normal commercial control. Stories of impoverished people selling their eyes or kidneys can be referred to as showing the dangers

----

4   It is unusual to spend so much time on one case in an essay. However, this is justified here because it is such an important case.

5   Sometimes the law is uncertain. Don't be afraid to say that the law in some areas is unclear.

of allowing bodies to become property. There are, therefore, both practical and theoretical concerns over the ownership of bodies. Third, there are practical issues for doctors and hospitals.[6] During routine surgery all sorts of bits of bodies are removed and disposed of, normally without thought. If they are all treated as property and there are restrictions on how they are dealt with this could seriously impede how a hospital works, without a corresponding benefit to patients. Most patients are not interested in seeing their seeping liquids or removed body parts again. So perhaps the courts are correct to be treading carefully. There may be a case for patients having property rights, or something like property rights, in relation to body parts in certain circumstances, but there are other circumstances where we would not want them. It will be interesting to see how the law develops.

> ### Common Pitfalls
> The *Yearworth* decision has set the law off on a new course. There is little point spending a lot of time discussing the previous case law.

QUESTION 24
Should the law recognise that separated body parts are property which can be owned?

COMMENTARY
This question addresses the key issue looked at in Question 23, but this time the focus is on the ethical issues raised. It is helpful to separate the practical and the theoretical issues raised, although these are often interlinked.

A mistake that is often made on either side of the debate is that the concepts of property or rights to bodily integrity are set in stone. It is possible to accept that something is property, but then put in place restrictions on how or which property rights be exercisable. So it would be possible to accept that body parts are property but then significantly restrict the ownership rights, so that it looks a very weak form of ownership. Similarly, it would be possible to use rights of bodily integrity, privacy and dignity to grant a set of rights that look very similar to property rights, without calling the body property. So make sure you show you are aware of the differences.

How to Answer this Question
   ❖   What is property?
   ❖   What alternatives to a property approach are there?
   ❖   Symbolism and concerns over commercialisation
   ❖   Need for positive claims
   ❖   Practical issues in hospitals.

6   Don't forget to raise practical issues as well as legal ones.

Answer Structure

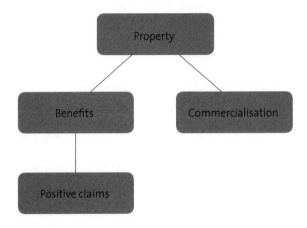

SUGGESTED ANSWER ------------------------------

Whether separated body parts should be treated as property has been an issue of considerable controversy over the last few years. Two trends in particular have led to increased calls for a recognition of property ownership. First, removed body parts can have considerable commercial value. In *Moore v Regents of the University of California* (1990) John Moore had his spleen removed. It was discovered by his medical team that the spleen had potentially beneficial properties.[7] They developed a cell line from it, which eventually sold for $15 million. It was said that subsequent products were worth several billion dollars. The research and use of his spleen was carried out without his knowledge or consent. His claim to be entitled to a share of the proceeds failed in part because he had no property claim over his removed spleen. Since that case, technological developments make it increasingly likely that body parts or cell lines will have considerable commercial value. The second change is a decline in paternalistic acceptance of the medical profession and an assertion of patients' rights. This might be seen in the Alder Hey scandal, where doctors who removed organs from children and then stored them for their own research or education purposes received considerable criticism from the press and public.

Most people in the debate over body ownership accept that people should have some legal control over removed body parts in certain circumstances. The issue is, however, what legal form this protection should take. There are two main schools of thought: one focuses on property rights, while the other focuses on other forms of rights.

....

7   This is a good case to use because it shows the issues around body ownership are not just academic but can be of practical significance.

Turning now to define the terms used: first, the notion of property.[8] Property involves a relationship between a person and a thing. It describes the relationship between a person and an object, in particular the legal rights and obligations. The rights that ownership provides are typically the right to use or enjoy the property; the right to exclude others from using the property; the right to sell or transfer the property to others. Full ownership will involve the use of all of these rights. But lesser forms of ownership may involve some of these rights. So a body part could be regarded as property even though the owner is not permitted to sell the item. An analogy might be drawn with a National Park, which is property owned by the state but which cannot be sold.[9]

Those who reject the property model prefer to focus on other human rights apart from property, such as rights to human dignity, privacy or bodily integrity. These, it is said, can provide protection for the interests people have over their separated body parts without the disadvantages of property rights. The right of human dignity is a notoriously opaque concept but it protects people and their bodies from being treated in a way which is seen as degrading or contrary to minimally acceptable cultural norms. The right to privacy protects the intimate space to develop one's personality and development. The right to bodily integrity protects our bodies from attacks from the outside. These definitions would all need considerable expansion, but in the debates below it will be shown how they could be used in certain contexts.[10]

We will now look at some of the particular issues in the debates. To begin with, some object to the property view on what might be regarded as technical grounds. This might take two forms. First, it is said that the notion of property requires a division between the owner and the thing owned. If the thing owned is the same as the owner then we cannot logically talk of a property relationship. That argument would carry considerable weight in an argument about whether we own our intact bodies and involve a debate over the extent to which we are our bodies. However, as the question asks about separated body parts there seems less difficulty in drawing a clear difference between the owner and owned in that context. Second, it is argued by some that property is produced (originally) by a person's labour. The reason why no one can claim to own the air is that it is not a product of labour. Similarly, our bodies are natural entities and should not be regarded as produced by labour. This kind of argument has developed from the writings of John Locke.[11] This argument could be replied to in two ways. One is to argue that in fact our bodies are the product of labour: we feed ourselves, keep ourselves healthy, etc., and that

---

8 Defining the central terms under discussion is a good way of starting an essay.

9 It is important to appreciate that just because something is property does not mean that all the consequences of full ownership follow.

10 Although the essay title asks whether bodies should be regarded as property, a good answer will consider the alternative forms of legal regulation.

11   J. Locke, *Works*, Amsterdam: Scientia Verlag, 1823, reprinted 1963.

takes work. The other is to deny that property must be the product of labour. Land may be owned even though it is wild and no work is done on it.[12]

Second, there is an argument over the symbolic message that is sent by the different ways of seeing the body. Opponents of the property approach (e.g. Rao[13]) argue that by regarding the body as property we are in danger of commercialising our bodies. Bodies become regarded simply as things to be used to achieve goals, rather than recognising the special place that they hold. Property rights are useful for protecting commercial interests, but not for protecting spiritual values. More concrete concerns are that vulnerable people can then be taken advantage of. Certainly there are plenty of reports of people in dire poverty selling their eyes or organs for money. Donna Dickenson's *Body Shopping* contains many examples of people being taken advantage of.[14] Supporters of property rights could respond by emphasising that one can support a property approach but still make the selling of body parts unlawful. As explained earlier, granting something the status of property does not wed you to the idea that you must allow the selling of body parts. Another response may be to challenge the idea that there is something wrong about describing people as property. People who are in dire need make money from all kinds of degrading activities (e.g. prostitution, pornography and unpleasant work) and selling their organs is no worse than these.[15]

A third issue concerns the *Moore* decision. Property rights supporters point to that decision as one where if property rights were recognised a much better system of protection would be available. Indeed, they argue that rights of privacy or dignity would not be of much help in the *Moore* case. They might lead to a requirement that his consent be obtained before his body product is used, and this might even lead to an award of damages if his consent was not obtained. However, they would not help him to obtain a share in the money made from his body part. We need to recognise that if a person's body part is used to generate money they should be entitled to a share in the money generated. Supporters of non-property rights will emphasise that their approach could be used to require consent to be obtained and damages to be awarded where it is not. But they will question whether in these cases a share in the profits is appropriate. Whether a person happens to have a profitable cell line is purely a matter of chance. It is the scientists who in fact do all the effort to change a spleen into a profitable commodity and it is they who should receive the financial recognition for their work.

A fourth issue is certainty. One of the benefits of a property regime is that we already have a well-established set of rules and principles which govern property. By contrast, the notions of dignity and privacy are rather vague. They are ill-defined and have a less

---

12 You can show your understanding of some of the philosophical issues here.

13 R. Rao, 'Property, Privacy, and the Human Body', 80 Boston *University Law Review*, 2000, 359.

14 D. Dickenson, *Body Shopping: the economy fuelled by flesh and blood*, Oxford: Oneworld, 2008.

15 It is an important point that the language used can be of considerable significance.

settled position in the legal world of regulation. This is a good point. Of course, it is not necessarily sufficient to outweigh all the negative consequences that opponents claim flow from the property approach.

A fifth issue is that it is said that while privacy and dignity might protect negative interests in the body they do not grant positive rights. In other words, they prevent people treating your body parts in particular ways, but they do not protect positive rights to do things with body parts in the way a property right does. In fact, here we are probably talking about the right to sell or buy body parts, as that is the most significant thing a person is likely to want to do to a body part. That brings us back to the debate above over the desirability of commercialisation of body transactions.

To conclude, the issue comes down to some profound questions about our relationships with our bodies. Do we regard our bodies as tools for us to use as we wish? In which case a property model gives individuals the greatest freedom to use their bodies as they wish and to dispose of them as they think fit. Or do we regard our bodies as having a sacred status, as being profoundly symbolic of humanity as a whole and therefore quite distinct from other forms of property? In that case the concepts of dignity and privacy may be seen as more appropriate tools for the legal regulation of body ownership.

> ## Common Pitfalls
> Don't make the mistake of assuming that if body parts are regarded as property then all of the rights attached to property necessarily must follow. It would certainly be possible to decide that body parts should be property, but that they cannot be sold.

QUESTION 25

Doctor Hai has three patients to deal with one morning. He operates on Sam, aged 4. He removes a small growth from Sam's cheek. Without obtaining the consent of Sam's parents he keeps the sample because he hopes to use it in a lecture he is due to give the following week.

During his operation on Michael, aged 60, Doctor Hai removes a cyst. He has an interest in cysts and has developed a large collection. Without obtaining consent he removes the cyst and adds it to his collection.

He also operates on Trudy, aged 22. While operating on her foot he is struck by her unusual hair colour. He snips a bit off and later sells it to a hair dye manufacturer for £2,000.

▶ Discuss the legality of Doctor Hai's behaviour.

COMMENTARY

This problem question requires a good knowledge of the **Human Tissue Act 2004 (HTA)**. There are other issues raised and these can be briefly mentioned, but the examiners' main focus seems to be on the **2004 Act**.

In the suggested answer, I have started by setting out the general legal principles, before looking at each case individually. That avoids having to repeat the basic legal principles each time.

How to Answer this Question

❖ Basic legal principles
❖ Sam: the growth: education?
❖ Michael: cyst: research
❖ Trudy: hair: human material: theft.

Applying the Law

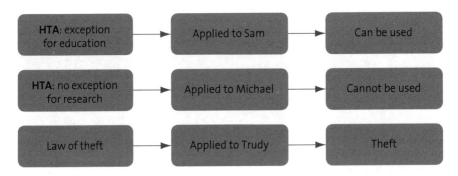

The main legal principles applied in this scenario are outlined here.

SUGGESTED ANSWER

Before looking at the individual scenarios I will set out the basic legal principles governing this arena.[16] A doctor who performs a procedure on a patient without his or her consent will be committing the tort of battery and even a criminal offence. The retention of material is governed by the **Human Tissue Act 2004**. **Section 1** sets out a definition of what can lawfully be done with relevant materials. Relevant materials are tissue, cells

---

16 If you are dealing with a problem question with different cases raising similar legal issues, it can be a good tactic to set out the general principles and then consider how they apply in each case.

and organs of human beings. Consent must be given to the storage for the use of the particular purpose in question. Consent for the storage of the material is required and the act must be for a Sch 1 purpose.

Turning first to Sam. We shall assume that Hai had consent to perform the operation on Sam. There is no question of a battery.[17] There is, therefore, no legal problem with the actual removal of the growth. Less straightforward is the growth. The issue concerns the retention of the growth on Sam's cheek. The first issue to address is whether that would be human tissue. It seems to clearly fall within the definition in s 53 ('tissue, cells and organs of human beings'). The second is whether he has stored the material from a living person. It seems from the facts that he has. Normally a person storing material for a Sch 1 purpose (which includes 'education or training') needs consent. However, the Act explains that there is a special exemption from the requirement to obtain consent in cases of 'education or training'. As long, therefore, as the purpose of the removal is education, Hai is acting lawfully and need not obtain consent. One slight query may be his desire to publicly produce the sample at a lecture, as that might amount to a public display, for which consent is required. However, as the schedule is put in terms of purpose a sensible interpretation would be what the holder's primary intention would be. Here any display is incidental to education.

Turning second to Michael. Again it seems there is no problem concerning the removal of the cyst: that seems to be lawful, assuming there is consent. The issue again concerns the storage of the material. As already explained, the Act requires consent where there is the storage of bodily material for a Sch 1 purpose.[18] However, in this case his purpose is only to store the material for his own interest. It seems, therefore, that s 1 does not apply. It is far from clear how the Act applies. Section 5(1) explains that there is an offence if without consent he does an activity 'to which s 1 applies'. So, the difficulty is in deciding whether the storage in this case amounts to an offence. One argument is that there is no offence committed because the purpose is not a Sch 1 purpose and so s 5 does not apply. It might, however, be argued that s 1 governs the storage of human material in general. The references to schedule 1 are incidental and do not affect the fact that s 1 applies to any removal of human material. It is not obvious from the wording of the section which interpretation is best. However, it may be helpful to remember that Michael's case is very like what happened in the Alder Hey scandal, which led to the passing of the Human Tissue Act 2004. It would be very surprising if the Act were interpreted in a way which meant that the Act did not prohibit the storage of material for the doctor's own interests.

....

17 If the examiner had wanted you to discuss this issue in more detail they would have indicated this in the question.
18 We have already explained this principle earlier in the answer and so there is no need to repeat the detail.

So it is suggested that **s 5** should be interpreted to apply to any retention by a medical professional without consent, unless that is permitted under the Act.[19]

The case of Trudy is rather different. First, there is an issue here over whether or not the removal of the hair is unlawful. Although, presumably, she consents to the operation on her foot, she did not consent to the removal of the hair. While consent to one procedure might be taken as consent to an inevitable part of the operation (*Davis v Barking, Havering and Brentwood HA* (1993)), here, however, the removal of the hair seems completely separate from any procedure concerning the foot. Consent to the removal seems neither express nor implied. Hai may therefore have committed the offence of battery and perhaps even an assault occasioning actual bodily harm (**s 47 Offences Against the Person Act 1861**; *DPP v Smith* (2006)). It will also involve the tort of battery. It might even be argued that he has committed the offence of theft (*DPP v Smith* (2006)).[20]

The storage of the material also seems to amount to an offence under **s 5** of the **Human Tissue Act 2004.** He does not have consent to retain the hair. What about the money that has been made from the hair – can Trudy have a claim for a share in the profits? This is unclear. It depends a little on whether Trudy can claim that the hair is hers. If so she might be able to bring a claim in conversion to request the return of property. Trudy could point to the decision in *R v Herbert* (1961), where it was suggested that hair is property. Indeed there is a long history of hair selling and it may be by common practice that hair is accepted as property. Alternatively she might point to *Yearworth v North Bristol NHS Trust* (2009) and the increasing acceptance of the possibilities of finding detached body parts as property, although in that case the court placed considerable weight on the fact that the material was stored at the request of and for the purposes of the individual.

QUESTION 26

'A person should be presumed to want to donate their organs on death, unless they have registered an objection.' Is this the law? Should it be?

COMMENTARY

Organ donation is a popular topic for examiners. A question along the lines of this one is typical. Because this is a popular topic it Is important to read widely so that you can make you're answer stand out. You should bring in articles or arguments that other students might not have mentioned.

---

19 Here we are acknowledging an ambiguity in the wording of the Act, but suggesting the most likely interpretation a court will take.

20 This paragraph is making good use of the case law.

Remember to read the question carefully. There is an important difference between live organ donation and post-mortem (after death) organ donation. You are asked in this question just to consider post-mortem, but if the essay had just referred to organ donation in general you might have been expected to refer to both.

This question asks you about a so-called 'opt out' scheme. You will need to explain that the current law does not adopt such an approach, but that some people argue it should.

How to Answer this Question

❖ The current law on organ donation
❖ The arguments in favour of an opt out system
❖ The arguments against an opt out system
❖ The alternatives: opt in; mandated choice; no choice.

Answer Structure

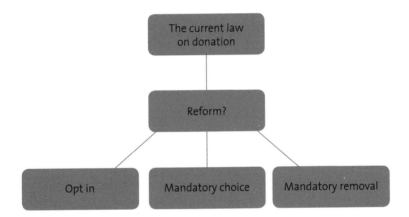

SUGGESTED ANSWER

There is much controversy over the current law on organ donation. Most people agree that there is a severe shortage of organs. The waiting list for organs is long and around 500 people a year die for lack of organs.[21] What is much debated is the extent to which this is due to a problem in the law, or whether the problem is rather located in social attitudes and concerns. Some people have proposed that we should move to a system of 'opt out' whereby people are presumed to want to have their organs donated on their death, unless they have made it clear otherwise. In this essay it will be explained that the current law does not adopt such an approach. It will be argued that the 'opt out' system should not be adopted, but rather we should move to a system of mandated choice.

---

21 This is a striking statistic which brings the issue alive.

The current law on donation post-mortem is governed by the Human Tissue Act 2004 (HTA). The Act focuses on the consent of the individual before death. If the deceased has made a decision about what should happen to their organs this must be respected. So the family cannot override the wishes of a patient to donate organs. If the deceased has not expressed a view then the doctors should consider whether the deceased has appointed a nominated representative to make the decisions under s 4 of the Act. If so, the representative can make the decision. If the deceased has not done that then the person who is in the closest 'qualifying relationship' to the deceased immediately before the death can make the decision. Section 27(4) of the HTA produces a list of relatives which are: (a) spouse or civil partner or partner; (b) parent or child; (c) brother or sister; (d) grandparent or grandchild; (e) a child of a person falling into paragraph (c); (f) stepfather or stepmother; (g) half-brother or half-sister; (h) friend of long standing. The person who is highest up the list can make the decision. So if there was a dispute between the husband and daughter of the deceased as to what should happen to her organs, the husband would win out. If two people rank equally (e.g. there are two brothers) then either of them can consent to the donation.[22]

As can be seen from this summary, the current law on organ donation does not fit the 'opt out model'. There is no assumption that a person wishes to donate. Indeed, quite the opposite, unless they make it clear they do wish to donate, it will be presumed that they do not.

The argument in favour of the current system is that we should not interfere with a person's bodily integrity without their consent. If a person has not consented, or appointed a representative to consent on their behalf, we can seek the guidance of relatives. The problem is that it seems many relatives are not willing to consent. It may be that in their grief it is easier to not make a decision (e.g. leave things as they are) than agree to a procedure. Also there is the fear that allowing removal of organs could be against the wishes of the relatives. Further, there is the difficulty that by the time relatives are found the organs are no longer usable. There has, therefore, been considerable attention paid to the possibility of reforming the law to presume consent or otherwise make it easier to remove the organs from those who have died. Perhaps the most popular option is 'opt out', the model proposed in the title of this essay.

An 'opt out' system has received support from the BMA and, while he was Prime Minister, Gordon Brown.[23] He commissioned an expert group to examine the issue (the Organ Donation Taskforce), which did not support the proposal. It has received recent support in the Welsh Assembly. One argument in favour of the proposal is that, as mentioned

---

22 Here we have provided a concise, but accurate summary of the law. You don't want to get bogged down in detail, but need to show you are aware of the basic principles.

23 Here we are able to show an understanding of some of the political background to the issues.

earlier, we know that, in fact, most people do wish to donate their organs but do not get around to registering. We can therefore assume that most people wish to donate and we can rely on those who do not to register their objections. Critics argue that this 'presumed consent' is a misnomer. In law consent is a positive concept: a doctor cannot assume a patient wants treatment if they have not given consent. A doctor who performed an operation without consent and said he presumed consent as most patients decided to undergo the operation would be found to have committed a battery. It is particularly wrong to presume consent in a society where we know there are some religious groups (e.g. orthodox Jews) who have strong objections to organ donations.[24] The Organ Donation Taskforce thought that the active consent principle needed to be maintained so that people have trust in the organ donation system and in the NHS generally. The consent principle, they argued, plays a central role in the doctor–patient relationship and we should not depart from it, even for the best of motives.

Another argument in favour of an opt out system is that a person who wishes to have their organs removed, but never gets around to registering, is having his or her wishes ignored. Indeed it might be asked whether it is a greater infringement of your autonomy to have your organs donated against your wishes because you never got around to opting out (which might arise in an opt-out system); or not to have your organs donated as you wished because you never got around to opting in (which is what happens under the current opt-in system).

A rather different argument in favour of the opt-out choice is that we should accept, as John Harris has argued, a moral obligation to donate.[25] Most people would happily accept an organ if it was required, so should they not therefore be required to donate an organ on death? The argument here is that we treat people's bodies as they ought to be treated (as a source or donated organs), although a person could opt out of that obligation if they have particular objections. However, the moral obligation might be questioned. Certainly parents are required to do what they can to help their children, but we are not required to assist strangers during our lives, so why should we be compelled to help children?

While these arguments are finely balanced,[26] I am concerned that we must not allow bodies to become 'State' resources to be plundered for the good of others, without the individual's express consent. The best way forward would be adopt a mandated choice approach. We need to find a way of compelling people to make a choice about donation. We know from surveys that a high percentage of people would be happy for their organs to be used for transplantation, but that they never quite get round to registering. Could we require, under threat of a fine, that people record their wishes on

---

24 An awareness of cultural differences which are relevant to the case at hand will impress the examiner.
25 J. Harris, 'The survival lottery', 50 *Philosophy*, 1975, 191.
26 Don't be embarrassed about admitting you find it a difficult issue about which to make your mind up.

organ donation? This could be done as a question on tax returns or benefits claims, or on medical records. Indeed it is currently done on applications for a driving licence. Of course, such a system would need some procedure to deal with those who still do not record their wishes. There seems to be much in favour of such a system and we could certainly do more to encourage people to make their wishes clear. The primary disadvantages would be the interference in liberty in compelling people to decide, and the costs in administering the system. However, that is a small price to pay if we are to save the lives of those needing organ transplants.

Before concluding we need to consider the radical suggestion that there be 'mandatory donation'. John Harris has argued that a person's organs should be removed after death whether the person or their relatives want that or not.[27] This argument could be supported in various ways. One argument is that, once a person has died, they have no interests. They have no feelings or wishes and so what happens to their body cannot harm them. They are no more. So no wrong is done in removing organs from a cadaver, even if the person while alive would not have wanted that. This argument is, however, controversial. Some commentators (e.g. Dworkin[28]) have argued that life can be seen as a story and our death and disposal of our bodies is the final chapter. Many people rightly want to have control of how their remains are dealt with, as part of their autonomy: it is their decision as to how their life develops. That is why so many people write careful plans about their funerals. Even if that argument is accepted it may be responded that our interests in determining how our remains are disposed of are tiny compared with the interests of the person who needs the organ, without which they will die. Indeed, as Harris points out, there is little dispute that autopsies are lawful, even if the deceased would not have approved.[29] However, the kind of consequentialist approach adopted by Harris would not receive widespread support. We do not generally allow the rights of one person to be overlooked in order to achieve a greater good.

In conclusion, nearly everyone agrees that it would be good to see more organs available for donation. The difficulty is finding the way to do this. The most desirable route would be to increase the number of people who choose to register to donate their organs. Although the numbers registered are increasing it seems there is still a substantial shortfall. The deaths of hundreds of people each year for lack of an organ, when probably there would be organs available from people who would have been willing to have them used, makes the current system hard to justify. Notably in Belgium, Italy and Greece the number of transplants greatly increased when those countries moved to an opt-out system; although Spain has managed to produce a dramatic increase while retaining an

27 Harris, op. cit.

28 R. Dworkin, *Life's Dominion*, London: Harper Collins, 1993.

29 Harris, op. cit.

'opt-in' system. The 'opt out' system, however, might undermine trust in the medical professional. It is a fundamental principle that things should not be done to our bodies without our express consent. The best option is to move to a mandatory choice system where everyone is required to choose whether they wish to donate their organs. We could use the taxation or welfare system if necessary to achieve this. By adopting a mandatory choice system people keep control of their bodies, while increasing the number of organs available for transplant.

Aim Higher ★

Bringing in comparisons with other countries can be helpful in debates of these kinds, although often cultural and social factors can mean that what works elsewhere does not necessarily work in the UK.

End of Life

Checklist ✔

You need to be aware of

- The legal definition of death
- When it will be a crime for a doctor to kill a patient
- The impact of the *Pretty* and *Purdy* litigation
- The law on assisting suicide
- The debate on whether there is a right to die
- The ethical issues which arise in end of life questions

QUESTION 27

How should death be defined in the law?

COMMENTARY

This question asks how death should be defined, but that is not a reason for not setting out the current law on the definition of death. Indeed, any question that asks 'What should the law . . .' can be answered by starting with a brief summary of the current law, before considering the alternatives.

A good answer to this question will set out the alternative definitions of death which have been promoted. It is probably best to prioritise your discussion. Some of the definitions have little support or are not really useful for lawyers. These can be mentioned, but spend more time discussing those definitions which are likely to be most useful.

Having set out the definitions, consider their benefits and disadvantages. You will want to indicate to the examiner that you are aware that reasonable people might disagree on this issue and highlight the factors that are likely to persuade someone to prefer one definition rather than another.

How to Answer this Question

- ❖ Background of the debate over death
- ❖ Brain stem death
- ❖ Stopping breathing
- ❖ The death of the organism
- ❖ Total cell death
- ❖ Desoulment
- ❖ Loss of conscious interaction
- ❖ Death as a process
- ❖ Non-definition
- ❖ Choose your own.

Answer Structure

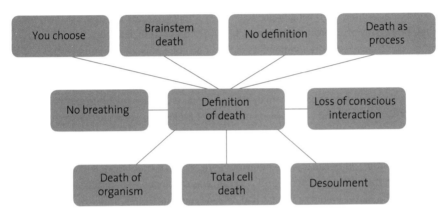

The issues to discuss in relation to the definition of death in this answer are outlined here.

SUGGESTED ANSWER

The definition of death has proved a problematic and controversial issue, but only in recent times. Death used to be all too common and often public. There would be little debate over whether a person was dead or not, and the exact time of death was not particularly important. However, technological changes have altered that. First, technologies can keep a person alive (or apparently alive) through artificial means in an astonishing array of situations. Then it can become far less straightforward to pinpoint the moment of death. Second, the issue of transplantation has made the time of death critical in some cases. It is important that organs are removed in a fresh state, as soon after death as possible, but that leaves open the issue of when death is. If death is defined as late in the process then the organs may not be suitable for transplantation.[1]

1   This paragraph sets out well the medical and social background to the issue.

Before looking at the alternative definitions that have been promoted we will look at the current law on death.[2] In *Airedale NHS Trust v Bland* (1993)Lords Browne-Wilkinson, Goff and Keith all accepted that the legal definition of death matched the medical one. In other words, the definition of death was to be determined by the medical experts, rather than a judge. In that case, and through to today, the consensus among UK doctors is that brain stem death is the best definition available (see also *Re A* (1992)). That will be explained shortly. Of course it should be noted that there is no reason why the law must follow medicine in these issues. There are some situations in which the law simply adopts a medical definition, but in others, for example the notion of insanity in the criminal law, the law sets out its own definition which does not match those of the medics.

Turning now to some of the alternative definitions. First, as already mentioned, brain stem death is the most popular in the UK. Indeed, the Department of Health has issued a Code of Practice for diagnosing brain stem death, implicitly accepting that it is the most appropriate way of ascertaining death.[3] A finding of brain stem death involves a conclusion that several key components of the brain stem have been permanently destroyed. This will mean that in effect a person's consciousness and ability to interact with the world have ceased. Their brain no longer works, or is only operating at a most basic level. Opponents of brain stem death argue that it equates the brain with the body. Walter Glannon complains that we are not just our brains. We are more than that. Just because the brain's functioning has ceased does not mean that the rest of the body is dead. It involves an understanding of being alive and being human which over-emphasises the role of the brain in our lives.[4] In response, Richard Veatch imagines a time when brain transplants are possible. If A's brain was taken out and replaced with B's brain, he argues, we would say that A had died. All their memories, thoughts and values would have gone.[5] But others would not agree with that.[6]

An alternative definition focuses on the end of breathing. This approach argues that it is the moment when there is a cessation of breathing which causes death. That was promoted by the Danish Council of Ethics. It will obviously appeal to those who see brain stem death as over-emphasising the importance of the brain. However, it is a problematic definition. Although a person may have stopped breathing, it may be possible through artificial ventilation to keep them alive. The test is likely to require, therefore, that there has been a permanent cessation of breathing, but it may be difficult to know whether that is so or not. A benefit of this approach is it that would match the expectations of the

....

2   Before getting into the theoretical debates, it is always wise to start with a summary of the current law.
3   Remember in practice doctors will follow the Professional Guidance issued by Professional Bodies and the Department of Health.
4   W. Glannon, 'Our brains are not us', 23 *Bioethics*, 2009, 321.
5   R. Veatch, 'Abandon the dead donor rule or change the definition of death?', 14 *Kennedy Institute of Ethics Journal*, 2004, 261.
6   In this paragraph good use is made of the academic writing.

person on the street, who is likely to see the stopping of breathing as indicating death and would be concerned with regarding a brain-stem dead, but still breathing, patient as alive.

A more extreme view is that we should regard the body as a whole organism and define death when the organism, as a biological entity, ceases to function. The biological approach might see ventilation, circulation and nutrition as central functions. We might say that once these stop there is death. Opponents argue that such views see bodies as machines, and fail to appreciate that life is not just about biological functioning but involves experiences, emotions and thoughts. An even more extreme version of this view is that the body is alive until every cell has died. The practical implications of this, if it were adopted in the law, would be problematic. They would mean that there would not be death until the body had started to putrefy. Most people would find that hard to stomach.

More popular would be a theory which argues for death as a loss of consciousness or social interaction. This would put death earlier in the process than the other suggestions above. The argument would be that what makes life valuable are the interactions with others and the world around us. Once those have gone there is no value left in life. So a person who is in a persistent vegetative state may be alive in a biological sense, but if there is no interaction with the outside world the life has lost its value and they should be regarded as dead. Indeed such an approach might even suggest that people with severe brain injuries are dead too. Opponents might argue that there is a danger here of merging the question of whether a person is dead and whether their life has value. It is one thing to say a person's life has lost its value; it is another to say they are dead – and we should not merge those questions.[7]

An approach to defining death in religious circles is the notion of desoulment. Death is when the soul leaves the body. Whatever its merits in theological terms, the major problem for the law is that it is not possible to determine when the soul (assuming that it exists) leaves the body.

For many people, including me, there are merits in many of the approaches above and there is no obvious answer to the question of when death occurs. Recently, commentators have sought to approach the question in a different way and we will discuss this next. First, some suggest that we should see death as a process. There is no one moment when a person dies (normally) and rather a person dies over a period of time. This has much to be said in favour of it, but is problematic for lawyers. We need a definition of death for the purposes of law regarding murder, transplantation and burial. We need to create, however artificially, a precise moment(s) of death. It might also be

7   It is always good to set out the advantages and disadvantages of a particular approach.

said to be psychologically necessary for medical professionals and for relatives and family for there to be an identified moment at which a person is dead.

A second answer is that we should let people choose their own definition of death (Bagheri[8]). This acknowledges that the definition of death reflects religious, moral and personal values and the law should not impose these on people. Each person should be allowed to choose their own definition. Presumably we might need to exclude some definitions of death if they caused public harm or health problems. But we might at least provide a range of definitions for people to select from. We would need also to produce a fallback position for those who have not indicated the form of death they wish to accept. The difficulty with this approach is that it suggests that the definition of death is entirely a personal matter and may overlook the interests of community, relatives and others in the appropriate regulation of death.

A final proposal (Chau and Herring[9]) is that we should side-step the question of the definition of death as a legal question. Instead we should break the issue down into a number of separate questions: at what time should organs be removed from a body; when is it permissible to bury a body; when can a ventilator be switched off? This might appeal to those who see death as a process. It might also enable us to recognise that one of the problems with the definition of death is that there is a whole series of issues tied up in it. By separating these we can more clearly decide how the law should approach the question.

> ## Aim Higher   ★
> The possibility of allowing people to choose their own definition of death is an interesting one. Have a think about any practical problems that might arise from that.

QUESTION 28 -

Assess the role that the doctrine of double effect has and ought to have in the law.

COMMENTARY

Here you are asked to discuss a particular issue in relation to the end-of-life debate: the doctrine of double effect. Notice that you are asked two questions: what role it has and what it ought to have.

8   A. Bagheri, 'Individual choice in the definition of death', 33 *Journal of Medical Ethics*, 2007, 146.

9   P.-L. Chau and J. Herring, 'The meaning of death', in B. Brooks-Gordan, F. Ebthaj, J. Herring, M. Johnson and M. Richards (eds) *Death Rights and Rites*, Oxford: Hart, 2007.

The essay will need to start with an explanation of what the doctrine of double effect is. It is worth noting that there is no agreement over the exact terms of the doctrine, but there is over its general impact. It is not worth getting too side-tracked by some of the finer philosophical aspects of the theory. Then it is a matter of looking at what the law says. To what extent is it reflected in the law?

Having set out the theory and considered whether it is part of the law, the next issue is whether it should be. There are arguments to be made on both sides. One point to watch out for is the assumption that if the theory is a good one in ethical terms it should be a good legal one too. The law cannot always exactly match the ethical test: it may be too complex for the law to use in jury trials or it may not give sufficiently clear guidance for professionals seeking to comply with the law.

How to Answer this Question
- ❖ Definition of the doctrine of double effect
- ❖ Consider whether it reflects the current law
- ❖ Pros and cons of the theory
- ❖ Will the theory work well within the law?

Answer Structure

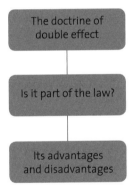

SUGGESTED ANSWER

It is generally agreed that a doctor who administers pain-relieving drugs to a terminally ill patient, foreseeing, but not intending, that the drugs will hasten death, should be regarded as acting lawfully. Indeed the statistics suggest that the administration of fatal doses of pain-relieving drugs is relatively common practice. The difficulty is in explaining why this practice is lawful.[10]

---

10 Remember to keep focused on the issue asked. For this question do not write everything you know about law at the end of life, but keep focused on the question.

The starting point for this issue is the law of murder. This explains that if a defendant has caused the death of a patient, with an intention to cause death or previous bodily harm, he or she is guilty of murder unless they can raise a defence, such as self-defence. The criminal law has defined intent to include two forms of intent. Direct intent arises where it is the purpose to cause the result. Second is indirect intent. In *R v Woollin* the House of Lords explained that, where a result was virtually certain and the defendant appreciated that, the jury could, if they wished, find intention. If we apply that to the case of a doctor administering pain-relieving drugs the legal position appears to be that if the doctor foresees it as virtually certain that death will be hastened then he or she could be found guilty of murder. This is where the doctrine of double effect is relied upon by some to argue that a doctor should never be found guilty.[11]

The doctrine of double effect draws a crucial distinction between intention and foresight. Supporters of the doctrine tend to argue that it is never permissible to intentionally kill someone. However, there are circumstances in which it is permissible to do an act which it is foreseen will cause the death of the patient. It is permissible whether or not the requirements of the double effect doctrine are satisfied. There are many versions of this and there are some subtle distinctions, but John Keown's has proved popular. He sets out the circumstances in which it is permissible to do an act which produces a bad consequence.[12]

1. The act one is engaged in is not bad in itself;
2. The bad consequence is not a means to the good consequence;
3. The bad consequence is foreseen but not intended; and
4. There is a sufficiently serious reason for allowing the bad consequence to occur.

Let us apply this test to a doctor providing pain-relieving medication. As to the first requirement, there is nothing wrong in giving pain-relieving medication in itself. As to the second, the doctor would need to show that he intended to relieve pain and not cause death. This second requirement means the doctor cannot intend to relieve pain by killing the patient. He or she must intend to relieve pain through the medication, but only to relieve pain. Third, there is the crucial requirement that the doctor foresees death but does not intend it. Finally, there is the rather vague requirement that there must be a serious reason to allow the bad consequence to occur. It might be argued in this case that the pain must be considerable before a life-shortening dose is appropriate. If a doctor gives a lethal dose of painkillers to cure a minor headache, that would not be a sufficiently serious reason.[13]

So is the doctrine reflected in the law? It seems fair to say that, although the courts have referred to the doctrine (e.g. in *Bland* and *Re A (Conjoined Twins)*), it has not been officially

---

11 This paragraph summarises well the current law.
12 J. Keown, *Euthanasia, Ethics and Public Policy*, Cambridge: Cambridge University Press, 2002.
13 Here we have shown we understand what the doctrine means, and have not just learned a definition 'parrot fashion'.

adopted as the law. As seen above, the *Woollin* test applies generally in relation to cases of indirect intention. The jury are left to decide whether or not to infer intention in cases where a result is foreseen as virtually certain. The jury could decide to acquit if a defendant satisfied the requirement of the double effect doctrine, but it does not appear they do. However, that argument is to assume that the *Woollin* test applies to doctors in the kind of cases we are discussing and that is not clear.

It is not clear because there have been some cases which suggest that a special rule applies. Lord Goff in *Bland* referred to an 'established rule' that a doctor could give pain-relieving drugs, aware they would shorten life. Similarly, in *R v Adams* (1957) and *R v Moor* (Newcastle Crown Court, 11 May 1999) juries were directed not to convict doctors in cases in which they were not intending to kill. One of the very few cases in which doctors have been convicted was *R v Cox* (1992), where a doctor gave a level of drugs which could not be justified on the basis of pain relief, but could only be explained on the basis of a desire to kill. It seems, therefore, that there is a special rule for doctors which allows them to administer lethal levels of drugs, as long as their intention is not to kill, but rather to relieve pain. That would be consistent with the doctrine of double effect. However, that does not mean that the law necessarily follows the doctrine exactly. Certainly it has never set it out with the kind of sophistication found in Keown's version.[14]

Should the law more formally adopt the doctrine? The first point to address is whether it is appropriate to draw a distinction between intention and foresight. To some the two concepts are clearly different. You might foresee that if you drink too much you will get a hangover, but that does not mean that you intend to get a hangover. You might foresee that people will think your outfit untrendy; that does not mean you intend them to do so. But is there a moral difference? It might be argued that there is, because whether a person acts with intention or foresight tells us much about the person's character. A teacher who tells a student that their work is poor, intending to cause them distress, appears malevolent; but a teacher who (justifiably) tells their student their work is poor, foreseeing that the student will be upset, is not acting improperly at all. To act with the purpose of producing a result is to tie yourself to a result and accept it as the rationale for acting. Acting foreseeing a result does not tie you to it in the same way. You are not suggesting it gives you a moral warrant for so acting.

Against these points is an argument that the line between intending and foreseeing cannot be drawn where the result is almost bound to occur. Andrew Simester gives the example of a head-hunter who cuts someone's head off to add to his collection of heads, but says that he did not intend to kill, only to add to his collection.[15] The argument is that where a result is bound to occur we are responsible for it and have to have a justification

---

14 It is helpful to refer to case law to show how the courts have applied (or not applied!) the doctrine.

15 A. Simester, 'Moral Certainty and the Boundaries of Intention', 16 *Oxford Journal of Legal Studies*, 1996, 445.

for it. If you drink too much, foreseeing a hangover, it is no defence to claim you did not intend to get a hangover. It is sometimes suggested we should see conduct in terms of packages. We cannot try saying we intend one part of the package but not the other. So when the doctor gives pain-relieving, life-shortening drugs, he or she cannot try to pick and choose which aspects he or she wishes to intend. The real question should not be what the doctor intended or not, but the more important question of whether the giving of the drugs was appropriate.

In conclusion, my view is that the doctrine of double effect is useful in determining whether a person has acted in a morally appropriate way or not. However, I am not convinced it is useful for the law. It places much weight on the state of mind of the doctor. That is notoriously difficult to know. If the doctor at the time of the injection of the drugs says his or her intention was not to kill, but rather to relieve pain, how can we know if he or she is telling the truth? That argument, however, might be made in any murder trial. More significant is the prospective power of the law. We need a law which will clearly inform a medical professional whether they may or may not provide lethal doses of drugs in a particular situation. The current law, and the doctrine of double effect, would say that it all depends on whether you are intending or only foreseeing the result. That does not really guide a professional. It would be far better to have clear guidelines as to when lethal levels of drugs can or cannot be administered, than to rely on the distinction between intention and foresight.[16]

> ### Common Pitfalls
>
> Students sometimes make the mistake of saying that, under *R v Woollin*, if the result is foreseen as virtually certain it is intended. That is not correct. The House of Lords explained that if the result was virtually certain and the defendant appreciated that then the jury *could* find intent, if they wished. But they did not have to.

QUESTION 29

Dr Albert is a passionate supporter of the right to die. He sees Ben, aged 74, who is suffering from a terminal illness. Ben asks Albert to 'give him something so that the pain will stop for ever'. Albert gives Ben a lethal dose of painkillers and Ben dies shortly after.

Dr Albert then sees Charlie, aged 17. His boyfriend has recently left him and Charlie is distraught. He asks Albert what is the best way to kill oneself. Albert tells Charlie the best way is to use a plastic bag. Later that day Charlie kills himself with pills.

---

16 Here the conclusion brings together the issues raised and focuses on the need for the law to be practically useful.

Dr Albert visits David, aged 83, who is suffering from dementia. David has fallen ill with a readily treatable condition. Albert decides not to offer him any treatment and David later dies from the illness.

▶ **Discuss the legality of Dr Albert's behaviour.**

COMMENTARY

There is a lot to discuss in this problem question. You are going to have to be quick to get through the material in the time available. There are also quite a few relevant facts missing, so for some answers you need to explain that it all depends on certain unknowns.

The first scenario, involving Ben, raises issues over euthanasia. Here you will need to explain the distinction the courts seem to draw between intention and foresight. In the second case notice that this is not a matter of direct killing because Charlie has committed suicide. However, there may be a charge of aiding and abetting suicide. The examiner will be impressed if you can show a good understanding of the recent reforms to the law in the **Coroners and Criminal Justice Act 2009**.

The third scenario is different from the other two as there is no obvious consent from the patient, but notice that this is also a case where there is an omission. You will need to explain the significance of the fact that the case involves an omission and a good knowledge of the *Bland* decision.

How to Answer this Question

❖ Ben: intention and foresight
❖ Charlie: murder? Assisting suicide? Reforms in the **Coroner and Criminal Justice Act 2009**
❖ David: an omission? Notice lack of consent. Apply best interests test.

Applying the Law

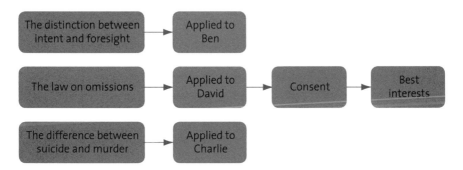

The main legal principles applied in this scenario are outlined here.

SUGGESTED ANSWER

Considering first the case of Ben.[17] The major issue is whether Albert has committed murder. The prosecution would need to show that he caused Ben's death. That appears to be proved on the facts. The second issue is whether Albert intended to kill Ben. Under the normal principles of criminal law, intention is restricted to cases of purpose. However, in *R v Woollin* (1993) the House of Lords accepted that intention can be found by a jury in a case where death or serious harm was the virtually certain consequence of the defendant's act and he realised this. In our case it is unlikely that Albert was acting for the purpose of killing Ben. If, however, he was intending to end his pain by killing him that might be regarded as equivalent to an intention to kill. Most likely, however, is that Albert's purpose was to relieve the pain, but that he foresaw that death might result. In that case he might fall into the *Woollin* category and it would be open to the jury, if they wish to infer intent. However, it may be argued that the case law on medical cases of this kind is rather different from the general rules of murder. Lord Goff in *Airedale NHS Trust v Bland* (1993) suggested that there was a special rule that if a doctor is administering pain-killing drugs he is not guilty of a crime, even though he knows that as a result of the administration the patient's life will be shortened.

There is another potential issue here and that is whether Ben has given effective consent to the treatment. We are not given the full facts here, but there may be claims that Ben was in such pain or so fearful that he was not able to consent to the treatment (see e.g. *Re MB*). There may also need to be an investigation into whether Ben had sufficient information to consent or whether Albert was negligent in not giving him enough information about the proposed treatment (*Chester v Afshar*). I will not explore these further as there is insufficient information in the question.[18]

Turning to the second question, Albert could face a charge of aiding and abetting suicide. The offence is found in **s 2** of the **Suicide Act 1961**, as amended by the **Coroners and Criminal Justice Act 2009**:

> (1) A person ('D') commits an offence if –
>
> (a) D does an act capable of encouraging or assisting the suicide or attempted suicide of another person, and
>
> (b) D's act was intended to encourage or assist suicide or an attempt at suicide.[19]

It seems that Albert may well have committed this offence. One of the amendments as a result of the **2009 Act** is that there is no need to show that the act of the defendant did in fact encourage or assist suicide; it just needs to be shown that the act was capable of

17 In this problem question it is helpful to deal with the three cases separately.

18 Examples from the case law are used here to illustrate the points being made.

19 Here we are showing the examiner we are aware of the recently enacted amendements to the law.

amounting to encouragement or assisting suicide. So the fact that the advice about the plastic bag was not actually used by Charlie does not matter, as long as it is accepted that it was capable of being encouraging or being assisting. The main issue at trial is likely to be whether Albert's act was intended to encourage or assist suicide. It is hard to see what other aim Albert would have had in saying what he did, unless he thought he was making a joke.

Following the decision of the House of Lords in *R (Purdy) v DPP*, the DPP has produced guidelines to assist prosecutors in deciding whether or not to prosecute for assisting suicide. In this case, given that Charlie is young, does not have a terminal or painful illness, and has not made repeated requests to die, it seems likely that a prosecution will be brought.[20]

Another possible claim in relation to Charlie is that Albert has acted negligently in not providing Charlie with advice about services which could help him with his suicidal feelings. The standard *Bolam* test would be used to determine whether he acted in accordance with a respectable body of medical opinion.

Turning finally to the case of David, the first point to notice is that this is a case of omission. A patient has an absolute right to refuse treatment (*Burke v GMC*). However, in this case David lacks capacity to make decisions for himself. This means that the decision must be made based on what is in his best interests (*Bland v Airedale NHS Trust*). Albert may try to argue that it was in David's best interests to die, but this is unlikely to succeed. Although there have been cases where the courts have accepted that the withdrawal of treatment might not be contrary to a person's best interests (*Bland v Airedale NHS Trust*), those have been in cases of the patient being in a persistent vegetative state or a similar condition. This case seems a long way from that and so it is unlikely the court will find it to be in his best interests to die. Albert may well, therefore, be guilty of gross negligent manslaughter. According to the House of Lords in *R v Adomako* (1995) this is committed where the defendant has acted in a negligent way which has caused a patient's death and the negligence was so bad as to justify a criminal conviction. A jury would need to decide whether the negligence was severe enough to lead to criminal penalties, or whether a finding of negligence in tort was sufficient. The courts have left this to be a question to be decided by the jury.[21]

QUESTION 30

Does the law recognise a right to die? Should it?

---

20 It is important to be able to apply the DPP guidance to the case you are discussing. Explain which factors in particular will be taken into account.

21 Notice we cannot provide a definite answer here, because it all depends on the jury's approach to the case. So, all you can do is set out the question the jury will need to consider.

COMMENTARY

Notice the two parts of this question. The first asks you to look at whether there is a right to die. You need to be careful here. The phrase 'right to die' is somewhat ambiguous. Does it mean that the state must not interfere in your decision to die? Or does it mean that the state must help you die? You need to set out the current law, especially the decision of the House of Lords in *Purdy*. When you summarise the current law there are two distinctions, which it is particularly important to bring out. The first is between assisted suicide and euthanasia. While assisted suicide can be unlawful (or at least it might not be prosecuted) euthanasia can never be lawful.

You are then asked what the law should be. This is a controversial issue, so try to present both sides of the argument in a fair way, even if you conclude one side's arguments are stronger.

How to Answer this Question

❖   The law on euthanasia
❖   The law on assisted suicide and the DPP guidelines
❖   The relevance of **the European Convention on Human Rights**
❖   The arguments based on autonomy
❖   The arguments based on sanctity of life
❖   Concerns about the vulnerable.

Applying the Law

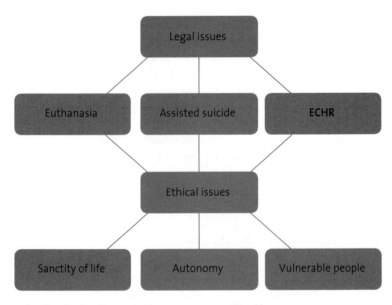

The core legal and ethical issues in this answer are outlined here.

SUGGESTED ANSWER -

The issues surrounding end of life are controversial. Many people are unhappy with the law. The recent Falconer Commission determined that a radical reform of the law was required.[22] In this essay the current law on a right to die will be summarised, before considering whether the law needs to be changed.

Before looking at the current law it is necessary to clarify what is meant by a right to die. One view is that this right is a liberty. In other words you have the right to be left alone. The State must not seek to prevent you committing suicide, with other people's help if necessary. In particular, the State must not make it unlawful to attempt to commit suicide or to assist in a suicide. The other view is that this right is a positive claim right. That you have the right to decide when you want to die and the State must actually help you do that. [23]

The current law makes it an offence to kill another person, even with their consent. This was confirmed by the House of Lords in *R(Purdy) v DPP* (2009) and in *R v Inglis* (2010). However, it is permissible for a doctor to decide not to treat a patient. Indeed if a competent patient refuses to consent to treatment it would be unlawful to offer them treatment, even if without it they will die (*S v St George's NHS Trust* (1998)).[24]

The position is rather different in relation to suicide. The **1961 Suicide Act** changed the law so that it is no longer a crime to commit suicide or attempt to do so. However, it is still a crime to encourage or assist someone to commit suicide. That offence was considered by the House of Lords in *R (Purdy) v DPP* (2009).

Debbie Purdy was suffering from multiple sclerosis. The disease was progressing and she foresaw a time in the future when she would wish to commit suicide. She would not be able to do this herself, but would require the assistance of her husband. Her plan was to travel to Switzerland to the Dignitas clinic with her husband, and to die there. She was concerned that if she did that her husband would face a charge of assisting suicide, under **s 2** of the **Suicide Act 1961**. **Section 2(4)** states that the consent of the Director of Public Prosecutions (the DPP) was required before any prosecution. Ms Purdy's legal challenge was that the DPP had failed to set out clear guidelines as to when he would or would not prosecute a case of assisted suicide.

Their lordships found in her favour and ordered the DPP to produce clearer guidelines. It is in the detail of their argument that the case finds its significance. The House of Lords unanimously found that making decisions about when and how to die involved **Art 8** of the **ECHR**, which protects the right to respect for a person's private and family life.

....

22 Here we are demonstrating to the examiner that we are aware of current events.

23 This paragraph shows a good awareness of the ambiguities surrounding a right.

24 Ample reference is made here to the relevant case law.

Decisions about how to die were deeply personal and could fall within the protection of **Art 8**. However, their lordships were also clear that the law could interfere in a person's **Art 8** rights as set out in paragraph 2 of that Article:

> There shall be no interference by a public authority with the exercise of this right except such as is in accordance with the law and is necessary in a democratic society in the interests of national security, public safety or the economic well-being of the country, for the prevention of disorder or crime, for the protection of health or morals, or for the protection of the rights and freedoms of others.

Their lordships accepted that the law could take the view that, in order to protect those who lacked capacity or other vulnerable people, the law could prohibit assisted suicide. That would be justified under **Art 8(2)** as necessary in the interests of others. However, two points arose from that. The first was that the intervention in the right to commit suicide had to be necessary. In other words a blanket ban on assisting suicide might be inappropriate. That is reflected in English law by the fact that **s 2(4)** of the **Suicide Act** acknowledges that the DPP is entitled to decide not to prosecute some cases. The second point – and this is more significant for the case – is that any intervention in the **Art 8** rights must be 'in accordance with the law'. The House of Lords referred to well-established European Court of Human Rights (ECtHR) jurisprudence that to amount to 'law' the regulations had to be sufficiently clear to guide conduct. They thought that in this sensitive area it was particularly important that the regulation be clear. The guidance issued by the DPP was found by their lordships to be too vague to amount to law. Therefore there was a breach of Ms Purdy's rights.

The significance of the Purdy decision lies in the fact that it is accepted that the right to commit suicide and receive assistance in suicide is protected under **Art 8(1)**. However, their lordships accepted that the law was entitled to make assisted suicide illegal in order to protect vulnerable groups under **Art 8(2)**. Their lordships could have gone further and noted that in fact the State is required to protect vulnerable groups from threats of harm, and so some legal protection of vulnerable groups who might be pressurised into committing suicide is in fact required by the ECtHR. However, the significance of the Purdy approach is that any restriction on who can commit suicide or be assisted in committing suicide must be justified under **Art 8(2)** as necessary and in accordance with the law. Indeed it raises the issue of whether making assisted suicide a *prima facie* offence is necessary in order to protect vulnerable groups. Would there be another way of regulating the area that would be just as effective as protecting vulnerable groups, but provide less intrusion into the rights of those who wish to commit suicide? I have in mind a system where someone seeking permission to commit suicide could apply to an expert panel for a certificate which would mean they would be permitted to have an assisted suicide.[25]

....

25 The legal response to assisted dying is dominated now by human rights arguments and so it is good to show the examiner you are aware of the issues.

Following the decision of the House of Lords, the DPP has issued new guidance on when he will or will not prosecute cases of assisted suicide. It is generally agreed that these provide much clearer guidance in which cases there will be prosecution. He lists sixteen factors that are public interest factors in favour of prosecution. These include that the victim was under the age of 18; that the victim did not have a clear, settled and informed wish to commit suicide; that the victim did not ask personally for the assistance of the suspect; and that the victim did not have a terminal illness or severe and incurable physical disability. It also lists thirteen factors against prosecution, including that the victim had a clear, settled and informed wish to commit suicide; that the suspect was motivated by compassion; that the victim was physically unable to undertake the act that constituted the assistance and that the suspect had sought to dissuade the victim from suicide. In issuing his guidance the DPP was clear that he was not seeking to make assisted suicide legal. Nor was he willing to provide guarantees that particular individuals would not be prosecuted. So the law on assisted suicide is in a strange state. Although it is a crime to commit suicide, there are plenty of circumstances in which the crime will not be prosecuted.

In *Haas v Switzerland* (2011) the European Court of Human Rights accepted that a person's decision to end their life was protected by **Article 8**. However, it rejected an argument that the state therefore had to help the person commit suicide, in this case by providing the medication they desired. **Article 8** in this context required the State to refrain from intervening, but did not require the State to help someone kill themselves.

Moving on to the ethical debates.[26] For supporters of a liberalisation of the law autonomy is the key principle. Writers such as Emily Jackson argue that people should be able to decide for themselves when they wish to die. Others might find their decision objectionable or even immoral, but they should not impose their views on other people. This right was to some extent recognised by the House of Lords in *Purdy*.

There are two main arguments that are used by opponents of a right to die. First, there are some who argue in favour of the sanctity of life. John Keown, for example, argues that it is a basic moral principle that it is wrong intentionally to kill an innocent person. That principle means that euthanasia, actively killing another person, can never be justified. Once we start allowing euthanasia we devalue the preciousness of life.[27]

A second argument used by those who oppose allowing assisted death is that if we allow people to be euthanised or assisted in suicide, vulnerable people will be pressurised into agreeing to be killed when that is not fully their wish. That may be because relatives keen on getting an inheritance pressurise them or it may be that the person is suffering from depression.

....

26 The essay asks you what the law is and what it should be and so you need to address the ethical issues.
27 J. Keown, op cit.

I suggest that the autonomy view is the best view. While I respect John Keown's moral stand he should not impose his morality on those who do not agree with it. Also, while we should be concerned about the vulnerable, we can put in place protective measures to make sure vulnerable people are not taken advantage of. The Falconer Commission came up with a powerful set of criteria which could protect the vulnerable person, such as requiring counselling and a waiting period. In the end I think each person's life is their own and they should be allowed to do with it what they want, including to end it.

Mental Health

Checklist ✔

You need to be aware of

- The definition of a mental disorder
- When a person can be detained under the **Mental Health Act 1983**
- How a person detained under the **Mental Health Act 1983** can be treated
- The significance of community treatment
- The controversy around the idea of 'dangerousness' in mental health law

QUESTION 31

Assess the grounds under which a patient can be detained under the **Mental Health Act 1983**

COMMENTARY

This is a pretty straightforward essay question. It requires you to set out the grounds for detention under the **Mental Health Act (MHA)**. You will want to go through three main sections dealing with admission and detention.

You are asked to assess these grounds and this requires a consideration of whether they are appropriate or not. Here it is useful to put the legislation in context. Highlight how it appears to contradict many key principles of medical law and ethics. It can also be helpful to draw on the **Human Rights Act 1998** as a way of challenging the current law.

How to Answer this Question

- ❖ Introduction to themes
- ❖ **Section 2 MHA:** admission to hospital
- ❖ **Section 4 MHA:** emergency admission
- ❖ **Section 3 MHA:** admission for treatment
- ❖ **Human Rights Act** issues.

Applying the Law

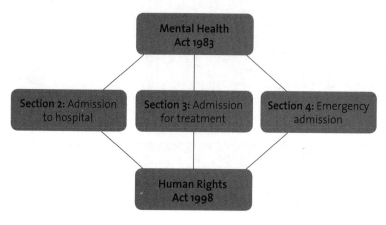

Factors to weigh up in relation to mental capacity and human rights law are outlined here.

SUGGESTED ANSWER -------------------------------

Medical law normally places considerable weight on a patient's autonomy and particularly the right of patients to be able to refuse treatment. As is well known, in *S v St George's NHS Trust* (1998) it was held that it was unlawful to perform a Caesarean section on a pregnant woman without her consent, even if without the operation she and her fetus would die. The **Mental Health Act 1983** provides a major exception to that principle.[1] It allows for the detention and treatment of patients who are competent, even without their consent. Having set out the circumstances in which this is permissible this essay will consider why this is permitted as an exception to the general approach taken by the law.

Section 2 of the **Mental Health Act 1983** permits the admission of a patient (P) for assessment. An application for admission can be made by either P's nearest relative or an approved social worker. The application must be supported by two registered medical practitioners. **Section 2(2)** sets out the grounds. It requires proof that P is 'suffering from a mental disorder of a nature and degree which warrants the detention of the patient in a hospital for assessment' and that P should be detained for 'his own health or safety or with a view to the protection of other persons'. Some of these terms need more explanation. First, mental disorder is defined in **s 1(2)** as 'any disorder or disability of the mind'. That is a very broad concept. **Section 1(3)** helpfully explains that a learning disability or alcohol or drug dependency cannot be used as the sole basis for having a mental disorder.[2]

....

1   The examiner will be pleased to see you putting the **Mental Health Act** in its broader legal context.
2   This paragraph provides a concise summary of the statute.

It is important to note that s 2 can only be used if their condition warrants detention for assessment. In *R v Mental Health Review Tribunal ex p Smith* (1998) it was explained that the issue for the court is not restricted to a consideration of the current manifestations of their condition, but it can consider their future behaviour.[3] So, if a patient is thought to suffer from a serious mental health issue, then they may be assessed, even though they are not currently posing a threat to their own or other interests. As s 2 makes clear, detention must be justified in the interests of the person's own health or the safety of others. So if detention is not restricted to cases where P poses a risk to others, it also includes cases where P is posing a risk to him- or herself.

Section 2 does seem very broadly worded. As the issue is about whether or not a person needs detention for assessment, the question is essentially whether there are concerns about their mental health. A suspicion that a person might have a mental health issue could be seen as sufficient to justify their assessment. The fact that s 2 only authorises a maximum of 28 days is seen by some as justifying a more relaxed approach to detention in the legislation. However, as the House of Lords in *MH v Secretary of Health* (2005) emphasised, a detention for assessment without consent infringes a patient's rights under Art 5 of the European Convention on Human Rights (ECHR). While a detention could be justified under s 2 the court will need to ensure that there was sufficient justification.[4]

Section 4 allows for admission to a hospital. A doctor needs to confirm that it is 'urgent necessity' for the patient to be admitted and detained. It also needs to be shown that waiting for the opinion of a section doctor to rely on admission under s 2 would cause 'undesirable delay'. Remarkably, the doctor does not even need to have expertise in mental illness. The laxness of the admission requirements should be read in the light of the fact that the patient can only be detained under s 4 for 72 hours. The section can only be justified as necessary to deal with emergency situations where there is no time to properly prepare a case for detention.

Section 3 provides for detention of patients for the longer term. An application for detention can be made by P's nearest relative or an approved social worker. There are three matters that need to be satisfied in order to justify detention under s 3.

The first is that the patient is suffering from a mental disorder of a nature which makes it appropriate for him or her to receive medical treatment in a hospital. Of course it is necessary to show that P suffers from a mental disorder. But more than that needs to be demonstrated. It must be shown that it is not possible for the person to receive treatment at home or in the community: they need detention in a hospital.

....

3   Remember where possible when discussing statues to refer to cases which have interpreted the statute.
4   Referring to human rights arguments can add another dimension to your essay.

The second is that it is 'necessary for the health or safety of the patient or for the protection of other persons that he should receive such treatment and it cannot be provided unless he is detained under s 3'. Notice that it is not enough to show that a person will benefit from treatment: it must be shown that their health or safety requires treatment. Another point worth emphasising is that it needs to be shown that detention under s 3 is required. Remember that if P consents then there is no need to use the MHA. This shows that s 3 should only be used where a person will not voluntarily agree to treatment.

The third is that 'appropriate medical treatment' is available to P. This is a very important provision. It means that s 3 cannot be used to detain someone if there is no treatment available. The significance of this is that it is possible to imagine a case where P suffers from a serious mental illness and poses a risk to others, but there is no treatment available to him or her. In such a case they could not be detained under the MHA. It is not surprising that this part of s 3 led to extensive debates in Parliament. Indeed it means that the most seriously ill patients cannot be detained under the Act. However, the requirement may not be as restrictive as it at first appears because s 145(4) explains that included within treatment is treatment which alleviates or prevents the worsening of the disorder or one or more of its symptoms or manifestations. So, if a patient's mental health means that he does not take care of his basic hygiene needs, that could justify a detention, even if treatment was not available for the actual condition. What, however, is clearly not permitted is a case in which P is to be detained simply for the purpose of housing and feeding him or her. There must be some form of care or treatment. However, given the inclusion of the symptoms, cases in which this element cannot be satisfied will be rare.[5]

Having now examined the grounds for detention a few general comments are in order. As already mentioned, the **Mental Capacity Act 1983** is a major departure from the basic principle that competent patients have a right to refuse treatment. It should be recalled that if the patient lacks capacity (as some with mental health issues will) then they can be treated in accordance with their best interests under the **Mental Capacity Act 2005**. So why is mental health a good enough reason to depart from this basic principle? There are two main suggestions. The first is that a person with a mental health issue lacks the capacity to make decisions for themselves. However, this is unconvincing. If they lack capacity then they can be dealt with under the **Mental Capacity Act 2005**. If people are being found to have capacity when they should not, then we need to reassess the **Mental Capacity Act**, rather than rely on the **Mental Health Act**. A second explanation is that those with mental health issues pose a special risk to others and it is important that their detention can take place to protect others. However, this is unconvincing. As Peter

---

5   Here we have set out the key legal requirements, but also explained some of the factors that will be taken into account when the court comes to apply them.

Bartlett has argued, there is no evidence that those with mental health issues are more dangerous than other people; indeed if anything, the evidence suggests they are less so.[6] In response it might be said that this may be true as a generalisation but if there is a particular individual who is known to be dangerous their detention is justified. The problem with such a claim is that we are not at all good at assessing who is dangerous. Even the best systems have a very high rate of 'false positives': those deemed dangerous in fact are not. The issue becomes whether we can detain a large group of people on the basis that some of them will commit crimes. Even if that were thought to be acceptable it may be that mental health is not the best criterion. Detaining large groups of those in low socio-economic groups might be a more reliable predictor. The fact that this would be utterly unacceptable means it should be on the grounds of mental health, too.

> ## Aim Higher ★
> The Mental Health Act marks a major departure from the principle that one cannot give treatment to a competent patient without their consent. Are there good reasons for departing from that principle in the mental health context?

QUESTION 32

How effective were the reforms in the Mental Health Act 2007?

COMMENTARY

The Mental Health Act 2007 was a much heralded piece of legislation. Indeed it was the result of a ten-year process seeking to reform the mental health laws. The end result was many fewer significant changes in the regime than had at one time been envisaged. Your essay will need to set out the main changes brought about by the Act, but should also consider how effective they have been. You could bring in a discussion of other reforms that were proposed but were not implemented.

How to Answer this Question

❖ The background of the Mental Health Act 2007
❖ The new definition of mental disorder
❖ 'Appropriate medical treatment' criterion
❖ Codes of Practice
❖ Community treatment orders.

---

6   P. Bartlett, *The Mental Capacity Act*, Oxford: Oxford University Press, 2005.

Answer Structure

*This mind map shows the main aspects of the **Mental Health Act** that will need to be discussed in this answer.*

SUGGESTED ANSWER

It was in 1998 that the government first announced that it had plans to reform the **Mental Health Act 1983** (**MHA**). However, after a series of reports and papers it was not until 2007 that legislation was finally passed. That reflects the fact that mental health law is a highly controversial issue. In this essay we will set out some of the key amendments made by the **2007 Act**. We will not be able to cover them all, but the following are some of the most significant changes.[7]

The first change was to introduce a new definition of mental disorder. Rather than trying to list the different kinds of mental disorder the **2007 Act**'s definition is simply 'any disorder or disability of the mind' (**s 1(2) Mental Health Act 1983**, as amended). **The Code of Practice to the Mental Health Act**, published after the 2007 reforms, gives some examples of what might be included, referring, among other things, to affective disorders such as depression and bipolar disorder and schizophrenia and delusional disorders.[8] The legislation makes it clear that learning disability or alcohol or drug dependency cannot be the sole basis for treating someone as having a mental disorder. So the legislation defines mental disorder in broad terms, and then excludes three categories of patients for whom it would not be appropriate to use the **MHA** apparatus. This is a desirable change in approach as it avoids doctors having to specifically identify the mental disorder in question before invoking the **MHA**. Given the difficulty in diagnosing specific mental disorders this seems appropriate.

The second change is an amendment to **s 3** of the **MHA**, which now states that a person can only be detained if there is 'appropriate medical treatment for them'. Previously the legislation had read that detention required proof that treatment would improve,

---

7   The examiner will understand that in an exam you do not have time to say everything you might want to say, but need to focus on the key issues.
8   Do refer to Codes of Practice because they will be used by the courts in interpreting legislation.

alleviate or prevent deterioration of their condition. To explain the significance of these changes, it is important to appreciate a key policy issue. The **MHA** legislation is designed to arrange for the treatment of patients who suffer mental disorders, even without their consent. It is not designed to arrange merely for their detention. So if a person is found to have a mental disorder but nothing can be done for them medically, they should not be detained under the **MHA**. That is because their detention would cease to be for their benefit, but would be for the protection of the public. If the **MHA** can be justified, it is justified on a paternalistic basis: the treatment will benefit the person and perhaps enable them to exercise autonomy in the future. However, if no treatment is possible then this justification cannot be used. The person is being detained to protect the public, but that should not be done under the guise of medicine. This treatability criterion therefore plays a central role in the law on mental health.[9]

The amendment to the treatability criterion has arguably made it a weaker protection for those with mental disorders. **Section 145 MHA** (as amended) defines treatment as 'psychological intervention and specialist mental health habilitation, rehabilitation and care'. It is the inclusion of care, which was not included in the original formulation, which may prove to be key. It may be argued that simply housing a person, feeding them and keeping them free from some dangers is caring for them. If so the treatability criterion could in effect allow for the warehousing of them. However, **s 145** does refer to special mental health care and so it may be that more than mere nursing care is sufficient. It remains to be seen how liberally this change to the wording is interpreted.[10]

A third change introduced by the **MHA 2007** was that it enabled the making of codes of practice. This is in line with other major pieces of health legislation such as the **Mental Capacity Act 2004** and the **Human Tissue Act 2005**. This enables the Department of Health or other official bodies to provide guidance in the interpretation of legislation in an accessible way for professionals. The **2008 Code of Practice** includes five key principles. These include that decisions under the act should be taken 'with a view to minimise the undesirable effects of mental disorder, by maximising the safety and wellbeing (mental and physical) of patients'. This is a welcome reminder that the Act must be used for the welfare of patients, and not the safety of the public. The second principle is the 'least restriction principle', which encourages those using the Act to rely on the consent of the patient. This is a welcome reminder that even though it is possible to use coercion under the **MHA** this should be avoided as far as possible. This is connected to the 'participation principle', which encourages patients to be involved in planning and developing their own treatment.

---

9 Here we are showing a good understanding of the theoretical issues, as well as the key legal provisions.
10 This is a smaller, more detailed, issue but it shows the examiner you are aware of the finer points of law.

A fourth major change made by the Act is the creation of a Community Treatment Order, under s 17A of the MHA. This order can be used after a patient is discharged, having been detained under the MHA. In effect it means that the release will be conditional. The Order can only be made if a clinician and mental health professional agree to make an order and the patient is suffering from a mental disorder of the kind which makes it appropriate for him or her to receive medical treatment and it is necessary for the patient; own health or safety or the health or protection of other people that the patient receives medical treatment. It must also be shown that the treatment can be provided with the patient needing to be detained in hospital. If such an order is made a patient can be recalled if there would be a risk to his or her health or safety or that of other people if the patient was not recalled. Critics complain that these orders can be used to continue to exercise control over patients even after they have been released from hospital. Supporters argue that they will enable more patients to be released from hospital.[11]

The 2007 Act also made amendments to the circumstances in which electro-convulsive therapy can be used and to the legal rights of a patient's nearest relative. It also provided for the creation of the Independent Mental Health Advocacy service which can assist in applications being made to a tribunal.

To conclude, the reforms of the 2007 Act are not radical, and certainly not as radical as was proposed in earlier drafts. The basic approach of the 1983 legislation continues unchanged. However, two of the changes in particular change some crucial boundaries. The amendment to the treatability criterion makes it easier to justify detaining a patient whose mental health can only be treated to a limited extent. Second, the use of community treatment orders provides greater control over patients with mental health issues who live in the community.

---

11   Here we are showing an understanding of the academic debates surrounding the legislation.

Medical Research

Checklist ✔

You need to be aware of

- The legal definition of medical research
- The meaning of consent in the context of research
- When medical research will be lawful
- The role of Research Ethics Committees
- When it is permissible to research using children and those lacking capacity

QUESTION 33

'Medical research contrary to public policy is outlawed.' Discuss.

COMMENTARY

This question involves a quotation to discuss. No author is provided, so presumably it has been created by the examiner especially for the exam. Do not assume that just because a comment is in quotation marks it is sensible. Sometimes examiners put down quite absurd claims for you to discuss. Certainly you should not be afraid to disagree with the quote provided.

In fact, this quote is not that absurd. Take time in the exam room to think about how the quote could be approached. In the suggested answer we go through the different ways in which medical research is regulated, considering whether all research which is contrary to public policy is outlawed and whether there are other reasons for outlawing medical research.

How to Answer this Question

- ❖ The need for consent
- ❖ Consent as a defence to assault
- ❖ Challenge studies
- ❖ Placebo studies.

Answer Structure

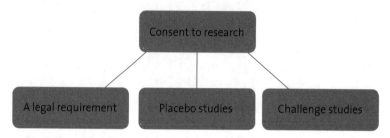

This mind map shows the main consent issues to discuss here.

SUGGESTED ANSWER

The legal regulation of medical research is made up of a patchwork of different provisions and regulations. In this essay we shall look at the different ways that the law regulates medical research.

A central principle is that for competent patients their consent is required before they can be involved in research.[1] Research without the consent of the participants is contrary to the public good and will infringe the human rights of the participants. The basic approach to capacity to consent is the same as applies generally in medical law. If there is a question mark over a participant's capacity to consent then the test for capacity in the **Mental Capacity Act 2005** will be used. Two issues in particular are likely to arise in relation to research. First there is a concern over duress. **Paragraph 26** of the **Helsinki Declaration** warns physicians running research projects to exercise great caution in using current patients in their research. **Paragraph 34** also warns that a decision to be involved or not involved in research must not affect the doctor–patient relationship. Despite these provisions there is concern that patients will fear that if they do not consent to be involved in the research they will be disadvantaged. The second concern is the amount of information that should be given to participants in research. There is guidance from the BMA on this issue which lists the information that should be given, in particular the potential benefits and harms that being involved could cause.[2]

There are special provisions that deal with those patients who lack capacity and these can be found in the **Mental Capacity Act 2005**. At first it might be thought unacceptable to involve in research those who lack capacity. However, if treatments are to be found for conditions such as dementia, this will have to involve research involving those who lack capacity. Indeed **ss 30–34** of the **Mental Capacity Act 2005** specifically provide for this. Crucially the project must be approved by the local Research Ethics Committee and must

---

1   This is the most important principle and so it is a good idea to start with it and discuss it at some length.
2   Here we have shown an awareness of the concerns raised by the case.

be connected to an impairing condition which the patient ('P') suffers from. The research must also have the potential to benefit P or to benefit people as a group who suffer from the condition P has. These provisions seem to strike the correct balance between the public interest in protecting those who lack capacity from being taken advantage of and finding treatments for those who lack capacity.[3]

A second principle is that under English criminal law the consent of a victim is not a defence if the harm caused by a defendant is actual bodily harm or more. This was established in *R v Brown* (1994), in which a group of men were engaged in consensual sadomasochistic practices. Their lordships controversially held that as the level of harm involved was actual bodily harm or worse their consent was no defence. There were exceptional cases where consent would be available, but there needed to be an activity in the public good, such as sport and medical procedures. It is not clear whether medical research trials could be included. There seems a good case for saying that they should be included in the list of exceptional categories, especially if the research is for worthwhile medical benefits. Perhaps reference could be made to **para. 21** of the **Declaration of Helsinki**, which suggests that the importance of the research outweighs the risks and burdens to the research subjects. This suggests that causing some pain in a project to find a cure for cancer may be acceptable, but causing the pain to find a cure for baldness may not. However, there must be a limit. A person cannot consent to be killed or even to having their life endangered (*R v Wacker* (2003)). Professors Hope and McMillan have suggested that research participants should not face greater risks than they would meet in ordinary life.[4] That, however, is a rather vague test. Some people engage in dangerous sports and regularly face serious dangers while others do not. Indeed, given that people are allowed to engage in highly dangerous activities such as rock climbing or boxing, why should the high-risk medical research participant have their choice less respected? It may be that they deserve greater leeway to participate in dangerous research.[5]

One controversial issue is so-called 'challenge studies'. These involve deliberately making people ill in order to study how a disease develops and different ways of treating it. This is seen as more controversial than giving a healthy person a trial pill to see if it has unpleasant side effects. The difference is that in a challenge study a patient is deliberately being made ill, rather than being given medication which only runs the risk of a harmful side effect. The Medical Research Council has supported research that involved deliberately infecting people with the common cold. It seems that challenge studies that involve this low kind of harm are acceptable; where, however, a more serious harm is deliberately caused then it becomes harder to justify.

....

3   Noting the delicate balance between these competing concerns will show you are aware of the difficulty the law faces in this area.

4   T. Hope and J. McMillan, 'Challenge studies of human volunteers: ethical issues', 30 *Journal of Medical Ethics*, 2004, 110.

5   This paragraph has combined case law and academic writing to discuss the issues in an effective way.

Another controversial issue surrounds placebo treatments. A placebo treatment involves giving a person what appears to be a pill, but is in fact a harmless substance, with no medically significant content. Typically where medication is being researched some in the sample will be given the trial medication, some a placebo and some no medication. The purpose of the placebo is to test what significance should be attached to the psychological effect of believing that you are being given medication. If the group who receive the placebo do as well as the group who receive the medication this suggests that it is the psychological effects of taking medication that are beneficial, rather than the medication itself. Why might this be ethically problematic? First, there is an issue surrounding consent. In such trials participants are normally not told that they may be taking a placebo, otherwise the trial would lose its purpose. If, however, participants believe they are being given a trial medication, are they being misled into consenting to the trials? One possibility is to try to fudge the issue and not tell participants directly that they will be taking medication, but this kind of half-truth-telling may not live up to the highest ethical standards that one might expect of the participants. The **Declaration of Helsinki** accepts the benefits of the use of placebos.[6]

A more controversial use of placebos arises where patients with a particular condition are currently using medication A, but are asked to be involved in a trial involving medication B. In that case, if they are given a placebo, rather than medication B, then they may be putting themselves in a worse position if they have given up medication A to be part of the trial. The **Declaration of Helsinki** suggests this may be permissible if there are compelling reasons, but it urges extreme caution.

To conclude, although the essay title asks when research is restricted in the context of public policy, there are difficulties in determining what the public policy is. On the one hand, there is a benefit to the public in there being as much research as possible into medical conditions. The more the better. On the other hand, a decent society will want to ensure that individual participants are not taken advantage of in the course of medical research. History teaches us the lesson of the dangers of using those who do not consent in medical research. Finally, there is the public policy of autonomy. If scientists wish to carry our research and participants are willing to be involved, should the State interfere? The current law strikes an uneasy balance among these aspects of public policy while at the same time striking an appropriate balance.

Common Pitfalls

Students often neglect to discuss the special provisions relating to children and those adults who lack capacity. They provide an interesting contrast to the regulation governing adults with capacity.

---

6   The **Declaration of Helsinki** plays an important part of the legal framework concerning research and it is well worth referring to it.

QUESTION 34

How does the law distinguish medical research and medical treatment? What is the significance of the distinction for the law?

COMMENTARY

This is an interesting issue which sometimes appears in exams. It is important because it explores the question of what is medical research and what is treatment. There are important legal differences between the two which need to be outlined in the essay.

A useful case to look at the issues is *Simms v Simms* (2003). In the suggested answer this case is used early on to highlight the issue at hand and to begin to set out the legal and ethical issues. Don't forget that the professional bodies may become involved here, as well as the courts.

How to Answer this Question

❖ Defining research and treatment
❖ Cases looking at experimental treatment
❖ Regulation of medicines
❖ Treatment of those lacking capacity.

Answer Structure

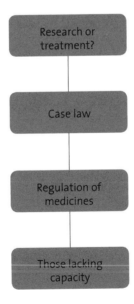

Research or treatment?

Case law

Regulation of medicines

Those lacking capacity

SUGGESTED ANSWER

This essay question focuses on the difference between research and experimental treatment. As we shall see, the distinction is crucial for the law. However, it is notoriously difficult to draw, as was well shown in the decision of *Simms v Simms* (2003).[7]

That case involved two teenagers who suffered from variant Creutzfeldt–Jakob disease (V-CJD). Their doctors proposed a novel treatment, which had not been tested on humans. The two teenagers were not competent to consent to the treatment, but both of their parents were willing to consent. The doctors were concerned about the legality of trying the treatment and so the parents sought a declaration from the court that the provision of the treatment would be lawful. The medical evidence was clear that without the treatment they would die. There was also unanimous evidence that the effectiveness of the treatment was unknown. The expert witnesses were asked whether they would be willing to use it on a patient and they were divided; however, they all agreed that it could not be described as irresponsible to use the treatment.[8]

Butler Sloss P, who heard the case, declared that it was lawful to provide the treatment. The two teenagers lacked capacity and so she determined that the key question was whether or not it was in their best interests to receive the proposed treatment. She held that it was. She noted that no responsible body of medical opinion thought it would be improper to provide the treatment. There was a 5 per cent risk of haemorrhage, but she thought that a reasonable risk to run given the gravity of the situation the patients were in. The proposed treatment was of benefit because it was unlikely to do them a serious injury and offered at least some hope of slowing down the deterioration in their condition. Even if the chance of success was slight it was worth taking. She accepted that the treatment was experimental and the risks were not fully known. However, given their condition was fatal and progressive it was worth using the treatment. She also attached considerable weight to the fact that the parents supported the use of the treatment.

This case shows how there is no firm line between treatment which is experimental, and research. It is a crucial distinction in terms of the law. If what is offered is treatment then the normal principles of medical law apply. Any challenge to it is likely to focus on whether the patient gave consent to the treatment and whether the offer of the treatment by the doctor was negligent using the *Bolam* test. We can see that approach being used in the *Simms* case. Butler Sloss P placed weight on the fact that there was no evidence that it was negligent to offer the treatment because experts agreed that it would not be irresponsible to offer it. She also found that, as the teenagers could not consent, the question was whether it was in their best interests to receive the treatment.

---

7   There is not much case law on this issue, so it is worth discussing, at length, the little there is.

8   Although normally you would not want to spend this much time setting out the facts of the case, as this is a leading case, it is important to explain its background.

If, however, the treatment is research then the legal regime becomes rather different. First, the Research Governance Framework applies to all NHS or Department of Health Research. This provides a broad range of regulations governing the practice. Second, the research must be approved in advance by the research ethics committee. This will consider a broad range of factors, including whether there are adequate arrangements to ensure that the full consent of participants is met; whether the legal requirements will be satisfied; whether the study has a scientific validity; whether the research will cause the participants undue pain or discomfort and whether any pain or discomfort is in proportion to the benefits of the research; whether there are adequate arrangements for the care and protection of participants; whether participants' rights of confidentiality will be protected; and the impact of the research on the wider community. Research is only permitted if it is approved by the Research Ethics Committee and complies with any requirements the committee imposes.[9]

In the case of research involving medicine, then the **Medicines for Human Use (Clinical Trials) Regulations 2004** must be satisfied. This requires the approval of the Medicines and Health Products Regulatory Agency of any testing involving new drugs. It must also comply with nine principles set out in the regulations. These include the key principle that: 'The rights, safety and well-being of the trial subjects shall prevail over the interests of science and society.'

There are special legal requirements where the research involves children or those who lack mental capacity. In the case of those who lack mental capacity there are restrictions imposed on their involvement in medical research set out in **ss 30–34 Mental Capacity Act 2005**. In particular this restricts the kind of research that can be conducted. It must either benefit the individual or provide assistance in the treatment of people suffering a similar condition to the one the individual suffers from. Even then, the risk to the individual must be minimal and it must not interfere in their freedom, action or privacy in a significant way. In relation to children, there are doubts over whether parents can exercise parental responsibility to give consent for the involvement of children in research which offers no direct benefit to the participants. This is because parents must make decisions on behalf of children based solely on what is in the child's welfare. However, research involving children which does not directly benefit the participants does take place. It may be that the courts would accept an argument that it is to the child's benefit to participate in socially beneficial activities. Nevertheless, the legality of the practice is uncertain.[10]

As we have seen in this discussion, considerable significance is attached to the distinction between research and treatment. The regulation of treatment is intense and there are very strict restrictions when it comes to research on those lacking capacity. Yet the

---

9   The role of Research Ethics Committees is key for this topic and they must be considered.
10   The examiner will be pleased to see you are aware that not everyone is an adult or has mental capacity.

distinction is not an easy one to draw. In the *Simms* case the treatment was unknown and in effect the teenagers were being used as human guinea pigs. The most obvious ground for the distinction is the extent to which the proposed course of action will benefit the individual. If the primary purpose is to benefit the individual it is suggested it should be regarded as treatment, but if the primary purpose is to discover information about the medicine or treatment, it should be regarded as research. As the *Simms* case demonstrates, even if it is treatment the courts will be reluctant to allow untried medicine or treatment to be used on patients unless the situation is extreme and there is no other alternative available.[11]

Aim Higher ★

This topic could be tied into the issue of autonomy. If a patient wants a treatment and a doctor is willing to provide it, why should anyone else be entitled to prevent the treatment from being given?

---

11 In this conclusion we have highlighted the key issues and considered how the issues may be addressed in the future, which is a good way to end an essay.

QUESTION 35

'Of the four great principles of medical ethics – autonomy, non-malfeasance, beneficence and justice – autonomy is the first among equals.' Discuss.

COMMENTARY

This essay is a very general one. There are quite a number of ways in which it could be tackled. You could seek to define the notions of autonomy, non-malfeasance, beneficence and justice; you could discuss whether they are the four great principles of medical ethics or whether there are others; you could discuss whether autonomy is the 'first among equals'; and you could consider various scenarios to show how the different approaches lead to different responses. To deal with all of the potential issues would take a whole book. Spend some time preparing for a question like this. What realistically can you cover and what are you best prepared to discuss? At the start of the essay set out what issues you are going to address and what you cannot discuss.

This essay mainly focuses on the ethical principles and so it is not one in which law will feature much, but it is good to show the examiner that you are aware of how ethical principles operate in real cases. So using one or two cases to highlight the issues raised will be well worth doing. Essays which are too 'airy fairy' may not go down well in a medical law exam.

How to Answer this Question

- ❖ The meaning of autonomy
- ❖ Discussing beneficence
- ❖ How significant is non-malfeasance?
- ❖ What is the relevance of justice?
- ❖ Is autonomy the most important principle?

Answer Structure

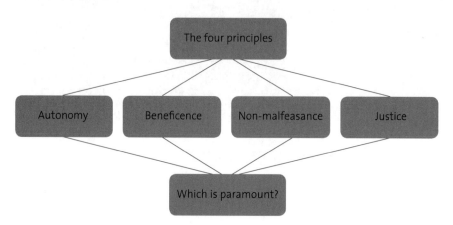

SUGGESTED ANSWER -------------------------------

In their highly influential book *Principles of Biomedical Ethics*, Tom Beauchamp and James Childress propose the four principles for medical ethics referred to in this essay question: autonomy, non-malfeasance, beneficence and justice.[1] However, for them these are four equal principles. This essay asks us to consider whether autonomy should be regarded as the 'first among equals' (a phrase used by Raamon Gillon).[2] To tackle this question I will seek to explain the four principles and then discuss whether autonomy should be regarded as more significant than the others. There will not be space to consider other ethical principles which commentators might wish to rely on or other approaches to ethical issues (such as those based on virtue ethics or ethics of care).[3]

Beauchamp and Childress believed that the four principles provided a 'common morality' which could be adopted worldwide. One of the reasons that their approach has received so much attention is that it can be supported by those approaching issues from a broad range of perspectives. A traditional Roman Catholic and a radical feminist might both look at an issue and find no difficulties in relying on these four principles to reach very different conclusions. Indeed Beauchamp and Childress argued that any particular ethical issue can be examined using the four principles. These may produce conflicting answers, but by balancing and comparing the application of the different principles an approach can be found. It is important to realise, therefore, that their approach is focused on giving a way to approach difficult questions, rather than purporting to provide a particular answer.

....

1   T. Beauchamp and J. Childress, *Principles of Biomedical Ethics*, Oxford: Oxford University Press, 2004.

2   R. Gillon, 'Ethics needs principles – four can encompass the rest – and respect for autonomy should be "first among equals" ', 29 *Journal of Medical Ethics*, 2003, 307.

3   While the 'four principles' approach is central to a discussion of medical ethics, the examiner will be pleased to see that you are aware that there are other ways of analysing the issues.

First, I will consider the principle of autonomy. In short, autonomy requires that we respect people's right to decide how to live their lives, unless doing so will cause harm to another person. Each individual should be allowed to decide what is best for them. This means that a patient should decide whether or not to accept a treatment offered by a doctor. It is seen as a firm rejection of paternalism, where the doctor decides what is important to a patient and what is best for the patient. Central to the notion of autonomy is that a person's decisions should be respected, however foolish they may seem to others. Hence if a Jehovah's Witness refuses a life-saving blood transfusion their decision should be respected, however inexplicable their decision may seem to others (as long as the patient is competent to make the decision: *Re E* (1993)). Not to respect a person's wishes and force unwanted treatment on them is seen by supporters of autonomy as a denial of their humanity and a breach of their human rights.[4]

It is, however, important to appreciate the limits on autonomy. First, it is primarily a negative concept. In medical law the right to refuse treatment is well protected. Notoriously in *S v St George's NHS Trust* (1998) the Court of Appeal held that a woman had the right to refuse a Caesarean section operation even though without the operation she and her fetus would die. However, the right to demand treatment is less respected. Even though a patient may request treatment, that does not, of course, mean that a doctor must provide it (*R (Burke) v GMC* (2004)). The doctor may determine that the requested treatment is not desirable or that a rationing decision means it cannot be offered. So although the exercise of autonomy to refuse treatment is strongly supported in the law, its exercise to request treatment is less so. That may be explained on the basis that, if treatment is refused, no one apart from the patient will be harmed. However, if treatment is insisted on that could affect others, it may affect the availability of resources for other patients; it may compel a doctor to provide treatment they think unsuitable.[5]

The second important limitation on autonomy is protected only for those patients who are deemed competent. A person who lacks capacity (e.g. a person with a serious mental illness) will be treated under the **Mental Capacity Act 2005** and be dealt with in line with their best interests. Similarly in relation to children, those with parental responsibility for them can make decisions on their behalf. So the autonomy principle has no real role where the patient lacks capacity to make a decision.

The second principle is of non-malfeasance. This states that a medical professional should not harm others. That sounds an obviously correct principle, as clearly a doctor should not provide harmful treatment to a patient. However, the principle makes it clear that it is not permissible to cause harm to one patient in order to benefit another. So

---

4   It is good to refer to cases to illustrate how the theoretical principle work out in practice.
5   The examiner will want to see that you are aware that there are exceptions to the principle of autonomy.

removing an organ from one patient in order to benefit another would infringe the non-malfeasance principle.

The relationship between non-malfeasance and autonomy is, however, complex. Taking the example of the organ removal, there would presumably not be a breach of the non-malfeasance principle if the patient consented. In such a case it might be said that the doctor should respect a patient's assessment that overall the donation would be good for them. But this raises the issue of how far that can be taken. If a patient wants treatment which is very harmful (e.g. removal of a limb) with no apparent benefit, should the doctor simply accept the patient's assessment that this is best for them?[6] Notice that if, even in a case like that, the medical professional should simply accept the patient's wishes then it seems the principle of non-malfeasance largely is assumed, not the principle of autonomy, at least for the purposes of competent patients. We should recall that autonomy does not guarantee the provision of treatment. Where a patient seeks harmful treatment with no redeeming principle any autonomy interest may be overridden by concerns over the impact of the treatment on the long term health of the patient and/or his family.

The principle of beneficence is that medical professionals should do good for their patients. Doctors are expected to put their patients' interests above their own interests. Of course this principle too must be read in the light of the autonomy principle. As we have seen already, even though a doctor might determine that a treatment would be beneficial, if the patient refuses it would be unlawful to provide that treatment. Further, simply because treatment might be beneficial to a patient does not mean that they have a right to demand it. It may be that a rationing decision means that it cannot be provided.

The final concept is the notion of justice. This requires that there be a fair and equitable treatment for patients. This includes the claim that patients should not be discriminated against. This is most relevant in the arena of rationing health care resources. People should not be denied treatment on the basis of their sex or their race. That is relatively uncontroversial. But what about age? Is it appropriate to decide that an organ should be given to a younger person before an older person because they will have greater use of it, or is that an ageist approach? Should the NHS spend greater resources on health issues facing younger people than older people?

The issue of justice should also be relevant in an assessment of public health issues. The fact is that there is wide disparity between the health of the wealthy and the less well-off, and between different ethnic groups. These disparities should be recognised as a major source of injustice.

---

6   Here a vivid example has been used to show how the theoretical issues might arise in practice.

One of the main criticisms of principlism (the approach promoted by Beauchamp and Childress) is that it provides us with no guidance on what to do with cases where these principles conflict. We have already mentioned cases where these principles might conflict. Indeed it might be suggested that it will be very rare for a medical professional to act in a way which could not be justified on at least one of the principles. Certainly any difficult case is likely to raise an issue involving a conflict between these four principles. So unless there is some kind of hierarchy the approach is of no use to those seeking to address difficult issues. It is this that leads some to suggest that, as the quote which is the subject of this essay argues, autonomy should be given a particular pre-eminence.[7]

That proposal should be treated with care. First, as we have already seen, autonomy cannot be given complete dominance. We cannot respect all requests for treatment. The NHS could not afford that. Second, autonomy could not be the only principle because we need to have principles that can be used in cases where autonomy is not relevant, such as in relation to the care of those lacking capacity. Third, there are plenty of areas of medical law where autonomy does not have direct application, such as issues around public health, forms of provision of health care or rationing. So we certainly cannot say that autonomy should be the only principle, and given the severe limitations on its application just explained, it often is not even the pre-eminent principle. Perhaps the most that can be said is that there are some issues of medical law and ethics where autonomy is the pre-eminent principle.

Aim Higher ★

Even when you are discussing ethical issues, refer to cases which are examples of where they apply. Also where possible cite authors who have written in support of particular ethical views.

QUESTION 36

Assess the contribution of feminism to medical law and ethics.

COMMENTARY

This essay title should only be answered by those who have a good understanding of what feminist thought has had to say about medical law and ethics. Don't assume that the sole feminist contribution is in relation to particular issues such as abortion. Nor should you assume that it involves simply seeking to ensure that men and women are treated in the same way.

7   It is good to show that you are aware that criticisms of principlism.

It is unrealistic to expect to cover all the ways in which feminist thought might be relevant to medical law, so pick a few that you feel happy discussing. One point you must bring out is that feminist thought is not restricted to arguments that the law directly discriminates against women in various areas. You will want to show the richness of the feminist approach.

How to Answer this Question

❖ Definition of feminism
❖ Direct discrimination
❖ Indirect discrimination
❖ Patriarchal constructs
❖ Ethics of care.

Answer Structure

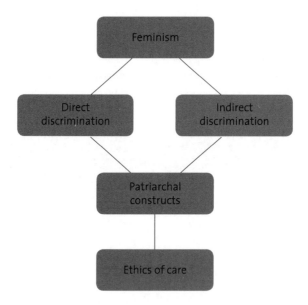

SUGGESTED ANSWER

Feminist approaches to medical ethics have had a significant influence on the development of the discipline. In this essay I will seek to set out some of the primary influences of feminist thought. In doing so it should be emphasised that there is not a single feminist approach to many issues. Indeed feminists often greatly disagree with each other.[8]

---

8   This is an important point to make. Don't assume that all those holding a broad theoretical perspective agree on all the details.

To start, it is necessary to explain what makes a particular approach feminist. In short this involves asking the gender question. For any issue we should ask what impact will the decision have on women and men? Feminists seek to be constantly aware of the potentially different impact that a decision might have on men and women. They are aware of the way that power has been used in the past and still today to work against the interests of women. Sometimes it will be obvious that a particular decision will work against the interests of women, while on other occasions it will not. Katrina George, for example, has argued that if euthanasia or assisted dying were made lawful more women than men would take advantage of it because women are particularly likely to feel they should not be a burden on others.[9,10]

Not surprisingly, therefore, much feminist writing has been exploring the way that medicine has worked to oppress women. Let us consider some examples. Medicine has been used to control women. Women who did not behave in a 'feminine way' were in the past classified as mentally ill. Childbirth has been presented as a medical issue, thereby making it something that doctors have control of. The same point can be made about abortion. There is no inevitability about regarding childbirth or abortion as medical questions, but doing so means that intimate aspects of women's lives are taken out of their control. Feminists have also pointed out the inequalities in health care provision. Some feminists have claimed that special attention is paid to diseases that are more common among men and that women's medical needs are too readily ignored.[11]

Another theme is that male norms are promoted. The ideal patient is seen as a man and there is the promotion of particular attributes. So a 'stiff upper lip' is regarded as desirable in a patient. There are plenty of cases in which a woman is regarded as 'too emotional' to have the capacity to make a decision (see for example *Re MB* (1997)). Further autonomy is generally regarded as a desirable characteristic and patients are assessed on their own. The idea of decision-making being a family or group venture is not recognised in medical law.

Cosmetic surgery provides a good example of how feminists might approach a particular issue.[12] To some feminists cosmetic surgery is an example of the use of medicine by men to exert power over women. The pressure put on women to conform to accepted standards of beauty and the significance attached to women's appearance is revealed by the fact that so many women resort to surgery. A proper feminist response to cosmetic surgery is therefore to attack the patriarchal forces that compel women to take the decision to undertake cosmetic surgery or even to make it illegal. However, other

....

9 K. George, 'A woman's choice? The gendered risks of voluntary euthanasia and physician-assisted suicide', 15 *Medical Law Review*, 2007, 1.

10 It is good here to refer to academic writing which are examples of the approach under discussion.

11 Give practical examples of the issues you are writing about, as well as discussing the theoretical points.

12 This provides an interesting practical example of the different approaches that can be taken.

feminists argue that this approach fails to recognise that women have agency and to respect their decisions. We should respect the decisions of women, even if we do not agree with them.

Feminists emphasise the importance of a lived-in reality for medical ethics. Decisions should be made based not on abstract theoretical principles, but on the basis of real lives. Carol Gilligan, looking at the ways boys and girls approach moral issues, distinguished between a male and female way of approaching difficult issues. Men preferred generally abstract principles as a form of moral reasoning (an ethic of justice), while women preferred to find solutions that worked for the particular individuals in the context of their particular relationships (ethics of care).[13] While later writers have not been as convinced by the extent to which these are male or female forms of reasoning, they have found it useful to distinguish different ways of approach moral issues which may be used to approach questions. Many feminist writers have preferred an approach based on ethics of care over an approach based on ethics of justice.

Ethics of care has produced one of the most influential aspects of feminist thought. This starts with a criticism of traditional ethical approaches which focus on autonomy and rights. These, it is claimed, are based on the image of an individual, isolated patient and fail to recognise that we live in interdependent, interlocking relationships. Rather than valuing individual decision-making and individual rights we should be seeking to find ways of promoting interdependency and mutuality. This means trying to find solutions that work in the contexts of the particular individuals and the particular relationships that they find themselves in. This approach tends to avoid using grand theories or principles of general application but rather to ask what approach will work best in the particular case. The approach seeks to emphasise the importance of caring and of dependency. It decries the way that medical law tends to emphasise the work done by doctors and medical professionals and overlooks the work done by those informally caring for others (see e.g. Herring[14]).[15]

> ## Common Pitfalls
> Don't assume that feminism is just about discrimination issues. It also provides new ways of approaching difficult questions.

---

13   C. Gilligan, *In a Different Voice: Psychological Theory and Women's Development*, Cambridge, MA and London: Harvard University Press, 1982.

14   J. Herring, 'Where are the carers in healthcare law and ethics?', 27 *Legal Studies*, 2007, 51.

15   Ethics of care provide an interesting way of looking at medical law and it is worth revising some of the literature on it.

QUESTION 37

Explain the difference between a consequentialist and a deontological approach to medical ethics.

COMMENTARY

This essay involves a discussion of the crucial distinction between a consequentialist and a deontological approach. It is well worth learning about this because the material can be used for many theoretical questions about medical law and ethics.

You will want to set out the two main camps, but be aware of the different variants within them. This can get very complex and so you need to keep the issues clear in your mind. Remember too to give practical examples of when the approaches will produce different results.

How to Answer this Question

❖   The meaning of a consequentialist approach

❖   The definition of a deontological approach

❖   When will they differ

❖   Criticisms of a consequentialist approach

❖   Criticisms of a deontological approach

❖   Is a middle way possible?

Answer Structure

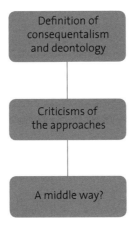

Definition of consequentalism and deontology

Criticisms of the approaches

A middle way?

SUGGESTED ANSWER

One of the major fault lines in ethics, including medical ethics, is between a consequentialist and a deontological approach to ethical debates. In this essay I will seek to explain these two approaches and discuss when they will produce different answers. I will also consider whether some kind of middle approach between them can be taken.[16]

The essence of a consequentialist approach is that one assesses the consequences of an act. If the act overall produces more good consequences than bad consequences then the act is morally approved, but if the act produces more harm than good then it is not. The consequentialist will normally reject any moral absolutes (e.g. killing is always wrong) because it is always possible to imagine a situation where more good than harm will result.

The essence of a deontological approach is based on certain basic moral principles. These involve moral rules: 'Thou shalt not . . .'. These cannot be broken whatever the consequences. The focus is, therefore, on the nature of the act, rather than its consequences.

At this point we will consider an example just to clarify the differences. Bob is given a new tie by his aunt for Christmas. He hates it. Should he tell her he likes it?[17] For a consequentialist it is necessary to weigh up the harmful consequences of saying he likes it with the benefits of telling the truth. Probably in such a case this will readily lead to the conclusion that lying is the morally better option. For a deontological approach there is a clear moral principle here: you should not lie. This means that, whatever the consequences, the truth must be told. The only possible argument here would be whether in this context this would be a lie. It might be argued that people don't take statements about presents at face value and so he might argue there is no deception here. Whether that argument has any merit would be a matter for debate.

Let us consider these approaches in a little more detail. In doing so we shall see that for each there is in fact a range of variants under the general headings consequentialist and deontological.

As we have already stated, a consequentialist would weigh up the good and bad consequences. That is probably how most people make decisions in their lives. If you are choosing which of two films to see you are likely to choose that which will give the greater pleasure. However, it is not, in fact, as straightforward an approach as might be thought. First, there is the difficulty in working out what is a 'good' consequence. Consider, for example, the facts of *S v St George's NHS Trust* (1998), in which a woman in labour refused to consent to a Caesarean section operation.[18] She was told that without

---

16 It is good to remember that issues need not be seen in 'black and white' terms and there may be middle routes available.

17 This is a homely example which explains well the differences. It shows the examiner you understand the concepts you are discussing.

18 Even though the essay is mainly about theory it is good to bring in some case law to give the essay a practical grounding.

the operation she and the fetus would die. It might be thought that the consequentialist approach would be straightforward. The harm is the harm to the woman caused by the operation, while the good is the saving of her life and that of the baby. Weighing these up, the harms outweigh the good. But what about the harm to her dignity: is that to count for anything? Do we just look at physical harm or emotional harm as well? We see the issue too in cases involving seriously ill babies and the issue arises whether we should discontinue their treatment. Is the focus just on physical pain or are there other effects that we take into account? Or consider the case of a person with body dysmorphic disorder, who wishes to have a limb removed because they do not feel it is part of their body. How are we to assess what is good for them: are they to decide what is good, or is that an objective value? If we are to use the individual's own assessment of what is good for themselves, that causes difficulties because we will need to interview people at length about their preferences before using the consequentialist calculation.

There is another difficulty here too. Take the body dysmorphic disorder case: how can we weigh up the emotional benefit that the person will gain from having the limb removed with the physical harm caused to them? This is a consistent problem for consequentialists: it requires weighing up a wide range of good and harm which are not readily compared. A consequentialist would probably respond that we must do the best we can to weigh these up. Critics suggest that this difficulty makes the consequentialist approach unpredictable.

There is even more to the unpredictability argument than that. We often do not know what the consequences of our actions are going to be. In trying to decide whether a patient should receive a treatment based on consequentialism we may be dealing with risks, some perhaps unknowable. This creates further difficulty for using the consequentialist approach.

Another uncertainty using the consequentialist approach is how far we should look at the consequences of our actions. Consider this case. A doctor diagnoses a man as being HIV positive. He does not want to tell his wife and forbids the doctor to tell her. Should the doctor nevertheless tell the wife? A straightforward consequentialist approach would involve looking at the harm done to the husband by the doctor breaking the medical confidence, along with the good to the wife of her being informed of the risk posed by her husband. But should we be looking further? If the doctor breaches the confidence in this case, will this deter other people who are fearful that they may be HIV positive from being tested or discussing issues with their doctors? Or if a doctor is considering whether a patient should receive a treatment, should the doctor consider the benefits and gains to the patient's relatives and friends, as well as for the particular patients?[19]

---

19 This paragraph highlights one of the problems with the consequentialist approach and provides a good example to illustrate it.

If we now look at the criticisms of consequentialism, one will already be apparent and that is that it is too vague to be useful: there are difficulties in knowing what the consequences of actions will be; whether they should be assessed as good or bad; and how to weigh them up. A second criticism is that it places no weight on the motives of the person acting. If a doctor carries out a gynaecological exam for sexual pleasure, the fact that the exam produced more benefit than loss may not satisfy us. Similarly, in assessing whether the man who told his aunt he did not like her present, we would think whether he did so intending to distress her was a relevant factor, yet it is not to be considered in a consequentialist approach. A third, and most popular, criticism is that it can produce results that people instinctively feel are wrong. If a doctor killed an elderly patient in order to use her organs to transplant into four patients who needed organs, he might try to argue that as a result he had produced more harm than good, but most people would find that result unacceptable.

As indicated above, for a deontologist there are certain kinds of acts which are good or right in themselves. Telling the truth is right because that is in its nature a good thing to do. It is not a question of the consequences of the action but the moral essence of the act. Immanuel Kant is a leading exponent of this kind of thinking. He argued for a basic principle which people should not use as a mere means to an end. It is never acceptable, according to Kant, to injure A solely in order to benefit B. That would be to use A as a means of benefiting B.[20] He would, therefore, strongly oppose the doctor who killed the patient to save four others. Deontologists refer to cases in history where great harm was done to groups of people in order to pursue the 'common good' (e.g. research by Nazi doctors on non-consenting people). They point out that such acts could be justified under a utilitarian principle.

For lawyers, a deontological approach could support the use of human rights. For example, under **Art 3** of the **European Convention on Human Rights** it is impermissible to torture someone. This is an absolute human right and so, however much good may be achieved by torture, it may still not be used.

Critics of deontology can make a number of points. The first is how we are to decide how these basic principles were determined. Some deontologists argue that there are some wrongs which are self-evident: the good of truth, knowledge, friendship, etc. are simply naturally good. But critics argue that this is all too vague. What might be obvious to one person is not to another. Unless we can find a way of producing a set of principles by which we all agree to abide, deontology faces a major problem for lawyers. That is especially so in a society which is as culturally, religiously and ethically diverse as ours. A second criticism is that deontology only helps with major issues, such as those involving

---

20 I. Kant, *Grounding for the Metaphysics of Morals*, Indianapolis: Hackett, 1993.

life and death. It offers no help if you are deciding what present to buy your friend. For such an issue consequentialism is more useful. Probably most deontologists would happily accept that. As long as a basic moral principle is not involved, they will generally be happy for a consequentialist approach to be taken. A third criticism is that it is provides too inflexible an approach. Remember the case of the present of the tie which the man did not like. In such a case, requiring him to be honest in the name of a high-minded principle seems too strict. Similarly, even if we accept that generally there should not be torture, what if torture will save a million lives? Surely there comes a point where the consequences of following the deontological rule are so awful we must be prepared to depart from it.

There are some middle approaches between the two. Some utilitarians have relied upon 'rule utilitarianism'. This approach recommends developing rules about conduct which generally produces good results. So we might say that doctors should breach medical confidences because generally speaking that produces more good than harm. This does not deny that there might be some cases where that is not true, but we need to have rules to guide our general behaviour. This might be particularly attractive to a utilitarian who is concerned about the uncertainty that a utilitarian approach can cause. A utilitarian adopting this approach would want to develop a way of dealing with cases where it seemed that following the general approach would not produce a good consequence.[21]

Deontologists too might seek a more moderate approach by accepting that there might be very special circumstances in which a deontological rule could be breached. So rather than saying you must never lie, this becomes you must not lie unless there are especially good reasons for doing so.

To conclude, there has been considerable debate between those who support a deontological approach and a consequentialist approach. The law probably takes a middle line between the two. As already mentioned, it is possible to find some strict deontological principles in the law: **Art 3** of the **ECHR** prohibits torture under any circumstances; it is a basic principle of medical law that a patient cannot be given treatment without his or her consent, whatever the harm that might flow. However, it is more common to find principles that might generally apply, but can be infringed: a doctor should generally respect medical confidentiality, but if necessary to avoid a serious harm, it can be infringed.

---

21   Here we are showing the examiner that we are able to look at the issue from a range of persepectives.

Index